the

wooden

box

PRAISE for The Boy on the Wooden Box

"Leon Leyson was a truly exceptional man and a gifted teacher. I will always be grateful to Leon for giving his testimony to the USC Shoah Foundation, which we will preserve in perpetuity so that generations to come can be inspired by his remarkable life. The world won't be the same without him, but we are fortunate to have this memoir to accompany his oral testimony"
—Steven Spielberg, Academy Award®-winning director of *Schindler's List*

"I loved this book and could not put it down. Leon Leyson's memories took me back to this other time, the other world where our childhoods were stolen, where overnight we became enemies of the state – to be destroyed, tortured, murdered – all because we were Jewish. Oskar Schindler has taught the world that one person can make a difference, and Leon Leyson certainly did that – by sharing his life and memories to the world."
—Rena Finder, another of Schindler's 'children'

"It is so important that these stories be told. There is a sad familiarity to them, and yet each child of the Holocaust is unique. My heart aches for the little boy standing on the wooden box but rejoices that he survived to tell us this unforgettable piece of history."
—Lois Lowry, Newbery Medal-winning author of *Number the Stars* and *The Giver*

"Reader's will close the book feeling that they have made a genuinely personal connection to this remarkable man."
—*Publishers Weekly*

"I loved Leon's story. It's honestly and simply told. It paints a vivid picture of life in Poland before WWII and an equally vivid picture of the hell endured under the Nazis. But it never revels in suffering. Readers will understand exactly why Leon was reluctant to share his story in later life and will like him even more for his eventual decision to share it. It's honest and it's heartbreaking but it leaves you with a determination to do better, to *be* better. I hope that's testament enough."
—*The Book Bag*

"Significant historical acts and events are here put into unique perspective by a participant."
—*Kirkus Reviews*

"In his book Leon asserts more than once that the key to survival was invisibility. Now the boy on the wooden box need be invisible no more."
—*The Daily Express*

"A privilege to read this moving memoir . . . poignant story has a blistering immediacy . . . This important book deserves to be widely read."
—*The School Librarian*

"An immensely powerful testament"
—Books for Keeps

SIMON AND SCHUSTER
First published in Great Britain by Simon & Schuster UK Ltd, 2013
This paperback edition published in 2014
A CBS COMPANY
Published in the USA in 2013 by Atheneum Books for Young Readers, an imprint
of Simon & Schuster Children's Division, New York

This book is a memoir.
It reflects the author's present recollections of his experiences over a period of years.

Simon & Schuster UK Ltd
1st Floor
222 Gray's Inn Road
London WC1X 8HB

www.simonandschuster.co.uk

Simon & Schuster Australia, Sydney
Simon & Schuster India, New Delhi

A CIP catalogue record for this book is available from the British Library

HB ISBN 978-1-4711-1967-5
PB ISBN 978-1-4711-1968-2
Ebook ISBN 978-1-4711-1993-4

Printed and bound by CPI Group (UK) Ltd, Croydon, CR0 4YY

1 3 5 7 9 10 8 6 4 2

the boy on the wooden box

Leon Leyson

Simon & Schuster
London   New York   Sydney   Toronto   New Delhi

To my brothers,
Tsalig and Hershel,
and to all the sons and daughters,
sisters and brothers,
parents and grandparents
who perished in the Holocaust.
And
to Oskar Schindler,
whose noble actions did indeed
save a "world entire."

—Leon Leyson

Leon Leyson's Route

DENMARK

Bal

Bremerhaven

Berlin

GERMANY

Gross-Rosen

Wetzlar

Prague

Brünnlitz

19 38

POLAND

Prewar borders
shown

Salzburg

AUSTRIA

PROLOGUE

I HAVE TO ADMIT, my palms were sweaty and my stomach was churning. I had been waiting in line patiently, but that didn't mean I wasn't nervous. It was my turn next to shake the hand of the man who had saved my life many times . . . but that was years ago. Now I wondered if he would even recognize me.

Earlier that day in autumn 1965, on my way to the Los Angeles airport, I told myself that the man I was about to meet might not remember me. It had been two decades since I had seen him, and that meeting had been on another continent and under vastly different circumstances. I had been a scrawny, starving boy of fifteen who was the size of a ten-year-old. Now I was a grown man of thirty-five. I was married, a US citizen, an army veteran, and a teacher. As others moved forward to greet our guest, I stayed behind in the background. After all, I was the youngest of our group, and it was only right that those who were older should go ahead of me. To be honest, I wanted to postpone as long as I could my disappointment if the man to whom I owed so much didn't remember me.

Instead of disappointed, I felt elated, warmed by his smile and his words: "I know who you are!" he said with a glint in his eye. "You're 'little Leyson.'"

I should have known Oskar Schindler would never disappoint me.

On that day of our reunion, the world still didn't know of Oskar Schindler nor of his heroism during the Second World War. But those of us at the airport knew. All of us, and over a thousand others, owed our lives to him. We survived the Holocaust because of the enormous risks Schindler took and the bribes and backroom deals he brokered to keep us, his

Jewish workers, safe from the gas chambers of Auschwitz. He used his mind, his heart, his incredible street smarts, and his fortune to save our lives. He outwitted the Nazis by claiming we were essential to the war effort even though he knew that many of us, myself included, had no useful skills at all. In fact, only by standing on a wooden box could I reach the controls of the machine I was assigned to operate. That box gave me a chance to look useful, to stay alive.

I am an unlikely survivor of the Holocaust. I had so much going against me and almost nothing going for me. I was just a boy; I had no connections; I had no skills. But I had one factor in my favor that trumped everything else: Oskar Schindler thought my life had value. He thought I was worth saving, even when giving me a chance to live put his own life in peril. Now it's my turn to do what I can for him, to tell about the Oskar Schindler I knew. My hope is that he will become part of your memory, even as I was always a part of his. This is also the story of my life and how it intersected with his. Along the way I will introduce my family. They, also, endangered their lives to save mine. Even in the worst of times, they made me feel I was loved and that my life mattered. In my eyes, they are heroes too.

ONE

I RAN BAREFOOT across the meadow toward the river. Once among the trees, I flung off my clothes, grabbed my favorite low-hanging branch, swung out across the river, and let go.

A perfect landing!

Floating along in the water, I heard one splash and then another as two of my friends joined me. Soon we climbed out of the river and raced back to our favorite branches to start all over again. When lumberjacks working upstream threatened to spoil our fun by sending their freshly cut trees downstream to the mill, we adapted quickly, opting to lie on our backs, each on a separate log, gazing at the sunlight breaking through the canopy of oak, spruce, and pines.

No matter how many times we repeated these routines, I never tired of them. Sometimes on those hot summer days, we wore swim trunks, at least if we thought any adults might be around. Mostly we wore nothing.

What made the escapades even more exciting was that my mother had forbidden my going to the river.

After all, I didn't know how to swim.

In winter the river was just as much fun. My older brother Tsalig helped me create ice skates from all kinds of unlikely materials, metal remnants retrieved from our grandfather the blacksmith and bits of wood from the firewood pile. We were inventive in crafting our skates. They were primitive and clumsy, but they worked! I was small yet fast; I loved racing with the bigger boys across the bumpy ice. One time

David, another of my brothers, skated on thin ice that gave way. He fell into the freezing river. Luckily, it was shallow water. I helped him out and we hurried home to change our dripping clothes and thaw out by the hearth. Once we were warm and dry, back we raced to the river for another adventure.

Life seemed an endless, carefree journey.

So not even the scariest of fairy tales could have prepared me for the monsters I would confront just a few years later, the narrow escapes I would experience, or the hero, disguised as a monster himself, who would save my life. My first years gave no warning of what was to come.

My given name is Leib Lejzon, although now I am known as Leon Leyson. I was born in Narewka, a rural village in northeastern Poland, near Białystok, not far from the border with Belarus. My ancestors had lived there for generations; in fact, for more than two hundred years.

My parents were honest, hardworking people who never expected anything they did not earn. My mother, Chanah, was the youngest of five children, two daughters and three sons. Her older sister was called Shaina, which in Yiddish means "beautiful." My aunt was indeed beautiful; my mother wasn't, and that fact informed the way everyone treated them, including their own parents. Their parents certainly loved both their daughters, but Shaina was regarded as too beautiful to do physical labor, while my mother was not. I remember my mother telling me about having to haul buckets of water to the workers in the fields. It was hot; the water was heavy, but the task turned out to be fortuitous for her—and for me. It was in these fields my mother first caught the eye of her future husband.

Even though my father initiated their courtship, their marriage had to be arranged by their parents, or at least seem to be. That was the accepted custom in eastern Europe at the time. Fortunately, both sets of parents were pleased with their children's mutual attraction. Soon the couple married; my mother was sixteen and my father, Moshe, was eighteen.

For my mother, married life was in many ways similar to how her life had been with her parents. Her days were spent doing housework, cooking, and caring for her family, but instead of her parents and siblings, she now looked after her husband and soon their children.

As the youngest of five children, I didn't have my mother to myself very often, so one of my favorite times was when my brothers and sister were at school and our women neighbors came to visit. They would sit around the hearth, knitting or making pillows from goose feathers. I watched as the women gathered the feathers and stuffed them into the pillowcases just so, gently shaking them so they spread evenly. Inevitably, some of the down would escape. My job was to retrieve the little feathers that wafted through the air like snowflakes. I reached for them, but they would float away. Now and then, I'd get lucky and catch a handful, and the women would reward my efforts with laughter and applause. Plucking geese was hard work, so every single feather was precious.

I looked forward to listening to my mother swap stories and sometimes a bit of local village gossip with her friends. I saw a different, more peaceful and relaxed side of her then.

Busy as my mother was, she always had time to show her love. She sang with us children, and, of course, she made sure we did our homework. Once I was sitting by myself at the table, studying arithmetic, when I heard a rustling behind me. I had been so focused on what I was learning that I hadn't heard my mother come in and begin cooking. It wasn't mealtime, so that was surprising. Then she handed me a plate of scrambled eggs, made just for me. She said, "You are such a good boy, you deserve a special treat." I still feel the pride that welled up within me at that moment. I had made my mother proud.

My father had always been determined to provide a good life for us. He saw a better future in factory work than in his family's trade of blacksmithing. Shortly after marrying, he began working as an apprentice machinist in a small factory that produced handblown glass bottles of all sizes. There my father learned how to make the molds for the bottles. Thanks to his hard work, his innate ability, and his sheer determination, he was frequently promoted. One time the factory owner selected my father to attend an advanced course in tool design in the nearby city of Białystok. I knew it was an important opportunity because he bought a new jacket especially for the occasion. Buying new clothes was something that didn't happen very often in our family.

The glass factory prospered, and the owner decided to expand the business by moving it to Kraków, a thriving city about three hundred fifty miles southwest of Narewka. This caused a great deal of excitement in our village. In those days it was rare for young people, really for anyone, to leave the town of their birth. My father was one of the few employees to move with the factory. The plan was for my father to go first. When he had enough money, he would bring all of us to Kraków. It took him several years to save that much and to find a suitable place for us to live. In the meantime, my father returned every six months or so to see us.

I was too young to recall exactly when my father left Narewka that first time, but I do remember when he came back to spend a few days. When he arrived, the entire village knew. My father was a tall, handsome man who always took great pride in his appearance. He liked the more formal attire of men in Kraków and gradually purchased several elegant suits. Whenever he came for a visit, he wore a beautiful suit, dress shirt, and necktie. That caused quite a sensation among the villagers, who were accustomed to loose-fitting, simple peasant clothing. Little did I know, those very suits would help to save our lives during the terrible years ahead.

My father's visits always felt like a holiday. Everything was different when he was home. Most days, given all that Mother had to do to look after my four siblings and me, meals were pretty informal. This changed when my father was there. We sat around the table with the serving dishes spread out before us. There were always a few more eggs at breakfast and a little more meat at dinner. We listened to his stories of life in the city, enthralled by his tales of the modern conveniences like indoor plumbing and streetcars, things we could scarcely imagine. We four brothers, Hershel, Tsalig, David, and I, were on our best behavior. We vied for our father's attention, but we knew our sister, Pesza, was really his favorite. Since she was the only girl in our family of rambunctious boys, that probably wasn't surprising. Whenever we siblings got into a minor altercation, I can remember it was never Pesza's fault, even though it might have been. When we teased her too much, Father intervened and reprimanded us. Pesza had long blond hair that my mother plaited into thick braids. She helped my mother around the house and was quiet and obedient. I can understand why my father favored her.

Often, Father brought us presents from the big city. The candy boxes he brought had photos of some of the grand historic buildings and tree-lined boulevards of Kraków. I used to stare at them for a long time, trying to imagine what it would be like actually to live in such a glamorous place.

As the youngest child, I always got the hand-me-downs: shirts, shoes, pants, and toys. On one visit my father brought us gifts of child-size briefcases. I saw my brothers with theirs and thought that once again I would have to wait until one of them passed his on to me. I really didn't think that was fair. This time I was in for a surprise. Packed into one of the briefcases was an even smaller one, just right for me. I was so happy.

Though his visits were only for a few days, my father always made a special time for me. Nothing gave me more joy than walking with him to his parents' house, with his friends greeting him along the way. He always held my hand in his, playing with my fingers. It was like a secret signal between us of how much he loved me, his youngest child.

My brother Hershel was the oldest; then came my brother Betzalel, known as Tsalig; my sister, Pesza; my brother David; and me. I thought of Hershel as the biblical Samson. He was big, strong, and feisty. My parents used to say he was a handful. As a teenager, he rebelled and refused to go to school. He wanted to be doing something more "useful." By that time my father was working in Kraków, so my parents made the decision that Hershel should join my father there. I had mixed feelings about this. I was sorry to see my big brother leave, but it was a relief also. He had been a worry for my mother, and, young as I was, I knew it was better for Hershel to be with my father. Hershel preferred city life and rarely came with Father when he visited us.

If Hershel was tough and headstrong, my brother Tsalig was in many ways his opposite. Tsalig was gentle and kind. Though he was six years older and had every reason to act vastly superior to me, his kid brother, he never did. In fact, I don't remember him once treating me like the nuisance I probably was. He even let me tag along with him on his excursions about town. A technical wizard, Tsalig was a superhero to me. There seemed to be nothing he couldn't do. He once built a radio using crystals instead of electricity to pick up broadcasts from Warsaw and Białystok and even Kraków. He made the entire apparatus, including the box that housed the equipment, and he figured out how to rig up a long wire antenna to get a signal. It seemed like magic to me when I put on the headphones Tsalig handed me and heard the famous trumpeter of Kraków marking the noon hour with his horn, hundreds of miles away.

It was my brother David, a little over a year older than I, who was my closest companion. I remember David telling me that when I was a baby, he would rock the cradle if I was crying. We were often together. Still, teasing me seemed to be among his favorite pastimes. He had a gleeful smirk whenever I fell for one of his pranks. Sometimes I felt so frustrated with his tricks, tears filled my eyes. Once, when he and I were eating noodles, he told me the noodles really were worms. He kept at it so long and remained so serious he finally convinced me. I gagged, and David howled with laughter. It wasn't long before we were best friends again . . . until David found another opportunity to pester me.

There were about a thousand Jews in Narewka. I looked forward to going to synagogue services with my maternal grandparents, with whom I was especially close. I loved hearing the prayers resonate throughout the building. The rabbi would begin the service in a strong, vibrant voice that soon blended in with the voices of the congregation. Every few minutes his voice would rise again as he called out a line or two, indicating where everyone should be in the prayer book. The rest of the time each member of the congregation was on his or her own. It felt as if we were one, but also that each of us had a personal communion with God. I guess to an outsider it might have seemed strange, but to us it felt utterly right. Sometimes when a Christian Pole wanted to describe a chaotic event, he would say, "It was like a Jewish congregation." In those peaceful times, such a comment wasn't meant in a hostile way, but as an affirmation of how strange we seemed to those whose religious practices differed from ours.

For the most part, Christians and Jews lived side by side in harmony in Narewka, although I learned early on that I was pushing my luck by walking down the streets in my usual carefree way during Holy Week, the week before Easter. That was the one time our Christian neighbors treated us differently, as if we Jews suddenly were their enemies. Even some of my playmates became my assailants. They pelted me with stones and called me names that were cruel and hurtful, names like "Christ killer." That didn't make much sense to me, since I knew Jesus had lived centuries before, but my personal identity didn't count for much compared to my identity as a Jew; and for those who seemed to hate us, it didn't matter when a Jew lived: A Jew was a Jew, and every Jew was accountable for the death of Jesus. Fortunately the animosity lasted only a few days out of the year, and generally in Narewka, Jews and gentiles existed peacefully alongside each other. Of course, there were always exceptions. The woman who lived across the street from us threw rocks at my Jewish pals and me just for walking on the sidewalk in front of her house. I guess she thought the very proximity of a Jew brought bad luck. I learned to cross to the other side of the street when I approached her house. Other neighbors were much nicer. The family who lived next door invited us over each year to see their decorated Christmas tree.

All in all, Narewka in the 1930s was a pretty idyllic place to grow up. From sunset Friday to sunset Saturday, the Jews of Narewka observed the Sabbath. I loved the quietness that fell as shops and businesses closed, a welcome respite from the weekday routines. After services in the synagogue, people would sit on their porches, chatting and chewing pumpkin seeds. They would often ask me to sing when I strolled by, since I knew a lot of tunes and was admired for my voice, a distinction I lost when I entered adolescence and my voice changed.

September through May, I went to public school in the morning and to *heder*, Jewish school, in the afternoon. There, I was expected to learn Hebrew and study the Bible. I had an edge on my classmates, since I had learned from my brothers, imitating them as they were doing their *heder* homework even if I didn't understand what they were studying. My parents enrolled me in the *heder* when I was five years old.

Roman Catholicism was the dominant religion of Poland, and religion was very much a part of the public school I attended. When my Catholic classmates recited their prayers, we Jews were required to stand and be silent. That was easier said than done; we were often reprimanded for trying to sneak in a whisper or a playful nudge when we were supposed to be standing like statues. It was risky to misbehave even a little bit, since our teacher was quite willing to tell our parents. Sometimes my mother knew I had gotten into trouble even before I arrived home in the afternoon! My mother never spanked me, but she had a way of letting me know when I had displeased her. I didn't much like that feeling, so for the most part, I tried to be good.

One time my cousin Yossel asked his teacher if he could change his name to Józef in honor of Józef Pilsudski, a Polish national hero. The teacher told him that a Jew was not allowed to have a Polish first name. I couldn't figure out why my cousin would want to exchange his Yiddish name—which in English means Joseph—for the Polish version, but the teacher's rebuff didn't surprise me. That was just the way life was.

I made my second home with our neighbor Lansman the tailor. I was fascinated by how he could direct the thinnest, most even spray of water from his mouth onto the clothes he was pressing. I loved visiting him, his wife, and their four sons, all of whom were skilled tailors. They sang at their work and in the evenings sat together making music, singing and playing instruments. I was mystified when the youngest son, a Zionist, decided to leave his home for distant Palestine. Why would he go so far away from his family and give up working and playing music with them? Now I realize his decision saved his life. His mother, his father, and his brothers all died in the Holocaust.

Narewka lacked most of what we consider necessities today. Streets were made of cobblestones or were unpaved; most buildings were constructed of wood and were only one story high; people walked or traveled on horseback or by horse and wagon. I still remember when the marvel of electricity reached us in 1935. I was six years old.

Every household had to decide whether or not to opt for electrical power. After a lot of discussion, my parents made the daring decision to bring the new invention into our home. A lone wire led to a socket installed in the middle of our ceiling. It seemed incredible that instead of a kerosene lamp, we now had a single glass bulb overhead by which we could read at night. All we had to do was pull the cord to turn it on and off. Whenever I thought my parents weren't looking, I'd climb on a chair and pull the cord, just to see the light appear and disappear as if by magic. Amazing.

In spite of the wonder of electricity, in most other ways life in Narewka remained as it had been for centuries. There was no indoor plumbing, and in the bitter winter the trip to the outhouse was one I learned to delay as long as possible. Our home had one large room that served as kitchen, dining room, and living room—all in one—and one bedroom. Privacy in the way we think of it today was entirely foreign to us. There was one bed, and we all shared it, my mother, brothers, sister, and I.

We collected our water from a well in our yard, dropping a bucket until we heard a splash, then winding it up full of water. The challenge was not to lose too much of the water as we lugged the bucket from the well to the house. It took several trips a day to meet our needs, so there was a lot of going back and forth to and from the well. I also gathered eggs, stacked wood chopped by Tsalig, dried dishes that Pesza washed, and ran errands for my mother. Most days I was the one who went to my grandfather's barn to carry home a pitcher of milk from his cow.

Our village at the edge of the Białowieża Forest was made up of farmers and blacksmiths, butchers and tailors, teachers and shopkeepers. We were agrarian, unsophisticated, industrious people, Jews and Christians alike, whose lives revolved around family, our religious calendars, and the seasons of sowing and reaping.

Those of us who were Jewish spoke Yiddish at home, Polish in public, and Hebrew in religious school or at the synagogue. I also learned some

German from my parents. It turned out that knowing German would prove more useful to us than we ever could have imagined.

Because Polish law prohibited Jews from owning land, as had been the case for centuries for Jews in Europe, my maternal grandfather, Jacob Meyer, leased his farmland from the Eastern Orthodox Church. He endured long hours of physical labor to support his family. He tilled his fields. He dug potatoes out of the earth with a spade and cut down hay with a scythe. I felt grand riding atop his horse-drawn wagon when it was piled high with bundles of hay at the end of the harvest. After my father left for Kraków, my mother increasingly relied on her parents for help. My grandfather frequently came by our house with potatoes and beets and other produce from his garden to make sure his daughter and his grandchildren didn't go hungry. Still, even with her parents' help, my mother had her hands full, since by and large she was a single parent raising a houseful of children. Just keeping us fed and in clean clothes and making sure we had the supplies we needed for school was a huge job. She never had any time completely for herself.

In Narewka everyone knew their neighbors and knew what they did for a living. Men were frequently identified by their occupation rather than by their last name. My paternal grandfather was known as Jacob the blacksmith, and our neighbor was Lansman the tailor. A woman was often referred to by her husband's name—as Jacob's wife, for example—while children were sometimes known according to who their parents or grandparents were. People didn't think of me first and foremost as being Leib Lejzon. They didn't even think of me as the son of Moshe and Chanah, but rather they referred to me as Jacob Meyer's *eynikl*, Jacob Meyer's grandson. That simple fact says a lot about the world in which I grew up. It was a patriarchal society, in which age was respected, even revered, especially when, as in my maternal grandfather's case, age meant a lifetime of hard work, of caring for his family, and of devotion to his faith. I always stood a little taller and felt a little more special when people spoke of me as Jacob Meyer's *eynikl.*

Every Friday night and Saturday morning at Sabbath services in the synagogue, I would stand next to my grandfather, bowing my head when he did and following his lead through the prayers. I still remember looking up at him and thinking how strong and tall he looked, like a giant tree shielding me. We always spent Passover at my mother's parents' house. Since I was the youngest grandson, I had the nerve-racking honor of asking the four questions traditional to the holiday service. As I recited the questions in Hebrew, trying hard not to make a mistake, I could feel my grandfather's eyes on me, willing me through my part. When I finished, I breathed a sigh of relief, knowing I had fulfilled his expectations. I felt lucky to be his grandson, and I always wanted to earn his approval and be worthy of his affection. I especially enjoyed spending the night with my grandparents all by myself. I would sleep with them in their bed, happy I didn't have to share it with my siblings as I did at home. How I loved being the center of my grandparents' attention!

Protected by the love and support of my family, I had little knowledge of the past persecutions that Jews in Narewka and other villages had experienced over the centuries, at the hands of first one ruler and then another. My parents had lived through attacks, called pogroms, in the early 1900s. Afterward many of Narewka's Jews left for America, among them my mother's brothers, Morris and Karl. Even though they knew no English, they believed that a better future was possible in the United States. A few years later Shaina, the beautiful sister, also sought a new life in America.

My parents had experienced war firsthand, the Great War of 1914–1918. No one before 1939 thought of it as World War I, since we had no idea that only twenty years later the world would again erupt in conflict. During the Great War, the German soldiers who occupied Poland were usually considerate of Poles, regardless of their faith. At the same time, in Narewka and many other villages throughout Poland, men were conscripted for forced labor. My father worked for the Germans on the narrow-gauge railroad that transported lumber and other supplies from our area to Germany. In 1918, when Germany was defeated, the occupying troops withdrew and returned to their homeland.

In retrospect, my parents and many others made a terrible mistake in thinking the Germans who came to Narewka in the Second World War would be like the Germans who had come in the First World War. They thought they would be people like themselves, men doing their military duty, anxious to return to their wives and children, and appreciative of any hospitality and kindness. In the same way people thought of me in relation to my grandfather and held certain expectations of me because of who my grandfather was, we thought of the Germans who entered Poland in 1939 in relation to those who had come before them. Logically, there was no reason for us to think otherwise. After all, what can we trust if not our own experience?

When I think back to the place where I grew up, the village that gave me so many treasured memories, I am reminded of a Yiddish song I used to sing with Lansman and his sons. It is titled "*Oyfn Pripetchik*"—in English, "On the Hearth." With a mournful melody, it tells of a rabbi teaching the Hebrew alphabet to his young students, just the way I was learning those letters in *heder*. The song concludes with ominous words as the rabbi warns:

> *When you grow older, children,*
> *You will understand*
> *How many tears lie in these letters*
> *And how much lament.*

In the evenings, when I sang this song with the Lansman family, those words seemed like ancient history. It never would have occurred to me those words were forecasting my imminent and terrifying future.

TWO

IT'S HARD TO IMAGINE a world without planes or cars, a world where people spent most of their lives in the same region and rarely traveled more than a few miles from their village, a world without the Internet or even the telephone. On the one hand, I cherish the memories of the small world where I lived the first years of my childhood. It was a world defined by the love and warmth of family. The predictable pattern of life made the rare moments of surprise especially memorable. As I think back to that way of life now so distant, I feel a sense of longing, particularly for my grandparents, aunts, uncles, and cousins.

My father's stories had given me a glittering image of the city of Kraków, three hundred fifty miles and light-years removed from the life I knew in Narewka. It must have been hard for Father to leave us for so many months at a time, hard for him to know the burdens he put on my mother. But my mother understood that my father was working to give us a better life and we had to be patient while he saved the money for us to join him. At last, in the spring of 1938, after five years of hard work and saving, he sent for us. I was thrilled. As an eight-year-old, I loved adventures. I knew the big city would hold plenty of them, and the thought of being with my father seemed like the best thing in the world to me. He had been away most of the time since I was three! So it was with excitement and not a hint of misgiving that I waved good-bye to my grandparents, aunts, uncles, and cousins, ready to begin a new life. I envisioned all my relatives and friends being there for me whenever I returned. Without a backward look, with my mother, brothers, and sister, I embarked on my first train ride.

I had never before been beyond the outskirts of my village, much less on a train. Everything about the trip was exciting: the sounds, the speed, the scenery rushing before my eyes. I was ready—or thought I was—for whatever would come next.

I don't remember exactly how long the journey was, only that it was long, several hours at least. I do remember every moment was fascinating. How enormous the world seemed, and we were just traveling a few hundred miles. When it grew dark, I was afraid I would miss something if I didn't keep my eyes glued to the window. It was well past eleven o'clock at night when our train reached the Kraków station. Father was there waiting, and we raced into his arms. We piled our luggage on the waiting cart and crowded up beside the driver. I was astonished that even at that late hour, way past my usual bedtime, there were streetcars and pedestrians everywhere. "We're almost there," my father assured us as we crossed the Vistula, the river that meanders through the city. As the horse clip-clopped down Kraków's cobblestone streets, I finally gave in to my desire for sleep. I had absorbed all I could for one day.

Minutes later we reached our destination. Our new home was in an apartment building at Przemyslowa Street 13, just south of the river. The building housed employees of the glass factory where my father worked. Our apartment was on the ground floor. Like our home in Narewka, it had only two rooms, a bedroom and a living room, but the living area in this apartment was much larger than in our previous home. What excited me most was the indoor plumbing. Before we collapsed into bed, my father led us down the hall to show us the bathroom we would share with three other families. He pulled a chain behind the toilet, and I watched, wide-eyed, as the water drained and the bowl refilled. Up to that moment I had thought the lightbulb was the greatest thing ever; but now, as I realized I would never have to make another late night trip to the outhouse, I decided the lightbulb and electricity were second to the toilet and indoor plumbing. As I pulled the chain and watched the water swish against the sides of the bowl, I thought this was about as extraordinary an invention as there could be. It had been a day full of wonders.

The next morning David and I set off to explore our new surroundings. Little by little, we ventured farther away from our building, first down the street, then around the block, and finally to the river where the Powstancow Slaskich Bridge connected our area to Kraków's main attractions: the traditional Jewish quarter of Kazimierz; the historic district of the Old Town; and Wawel Castle, the royal palace of kings and queens who had ruled when Kraków was the capital of medieval Poland. Pretty soon I felt brave enough to risk exploring on my own. All those scenes I had admired on the candy boxes were even more impressive in reality. I was especially drawn to Kraków's grand parks and historic buildings, such as the Old Synagogue, which dated back to the 1400s, and St. Mary's Basilica, a majestic fourteenth-century Gothic church that towered over the main square. It was at this church where, every noon, the trumpeter I had heard on Tsalig's radio played.

Every day was a new adventure, and I couldn't wait to discover what I would find around the next corner. Sometimes I would put my hand on a building just to make sure I wasn't dreaming. The hustle and bustle on the street made it seem like everyone had something important to do. Sometimes I tried to keep up with legs much longer than mine just to see where they were going. It was fun observing all the different kinds of shoes people wore and then looking up to see the face of the person wearing them. Sometimes I would stop in my tracks to stare at a department store window filled with lavish displays of merchandise, from clothing and jewelry to appliances. I had never seen anything like it. It was like being on a movie set or in an amusement park—although at the time I had no idea such places existed.

Our apartment was in a working-class, industrial neighborhood just a few blocks from my father's factory on Lipowa Street. There were lots of boys my age. Sometimes they made fun of me for my openmouthed wonder at sights they took for granted. They liked being the sophisticated city kids who could explain how things worked to the naive country boy. Occasionally, however, they stopped with me to look at whatever wondrous object had caught my eye.

Before long I had a few special friends, and we loved making up games. One of our favorites was to ride the streetcars that traversed the city. Since my new friends and I never had any money, we devised what we thought was an extraordinarily clever way to ride for free. We would hop onto the car at the end opposite from where the conductor stood. As he made his way toward us, collecting fares and punching tickets, we would plot our escape. We jumped off the streetcar just before the conductor reached us and dashed to the other end of the car to repeat our adventure, at least for a few stops until the conductor caught on to our scheme. I never tired of pulling this trick.

The fact that I was Jewish and they were not didn't seem to matter to my new pals. All that mattered was that I shared their sense of mischief and daring.

Kraków was not only a historic city but also a cosmopolitan and glittering cultural center, full of theaters and cafés, an opera house and nightclubs. My father's modest income didn't allow us any of those entertainments. The closest I got to Kraków nightlife was when I delivered love notes between a man at a cabaret and a woman who lived in the apartment next door to ours. The neighbor would give me fare for the streetcar, but instead of riding, I walked the short distance. When I reached the cabaret, I passed the note to the doorman. While awaiting the reply, I would peek inside, eager to see what drew people to go there night after night. I never got to see much, although I did hear lively Polish music. After a little while I would walk home, giving my fare to my mother, since even before the war, in my family, money was scarce.

My father was glad to have his family with him. He proudly introduced us around his glass factory, and he always welcomed David and me at his work. If he was busy with a project, he set us up with some time-consuming assignment such as sawing a thick log in half. There was no real point to the task, but my father showered us with compliments when the two sides dropped to the floor. A skilled tool and die maker, my father made replacement parts for broken machines and crafted forms for the glass bottles the company produced. As an expert machinist he was sought after by many factory owners in the area. His pride in his work spilled over into our home, where he was clearly the king of the castle, even if the castle was just a modest apartment. My mother tried to meet his every need; we children came second.

In the years we had been apart, my oldest brother, Hershel, had matured under my father's tutelage. He had settled down, found work, and started saving money. Instead of being disruptive, Hershel was now considerate and responsible. He also had a girlfriend, so, though he was once again part of our daily lives, we hardly ever saw him.

Life in Kraków began to be familiar. We focused on getting settled, making a home, and enjoying being together. When we began to hear about the unrest and violence in Germany, it was disturbing; but we had our hands full with daily life, and that was all we could manage. In September 1938 we celebrated Rosh Hashanah, the beginning of the Jewish year, and observed Yom Kippur, the Day of Atonement, in a beautiful Reform synagogue, one of more than a hundred synagogues scattered throughout the city. There were about 60,000 Jews in Kraków, approximately one quarter of the city's population. To me, it seemed like we were fully integrated into the city's life. Now, in retrospect, I realize that there were signs pointing to troubled times ahead.

At my new elementary school, an enormous place with hundreds of children from my neighborhood, my fourth-grade teacher singled me out one day. He addressed me as Mosiek, the diminutive for Moshe. At first I was impressed. I thought that this man must know my father, Moshe, and realize that I am his son. If anything, I felt proud that my dad was so well known. Only later did I learn that the teacher didn't know my father at all and that the name Mosiek, "little Moses," was an insult reserved for any Jewish boy, regardless of his father's name. Then I felt foolish for being so gullible.

Still, my life remained absorbed by school and play and chores, running to the bakery to buy a loaf of bread or to the cobbler to pick up shoes that had been mended. But the worrisome reports of what was happening in Germany became harder and harder to avoid.

October 1938 began with disturbing news. Newspapers, radio broadcasts, and conversations everywhere were full of stories about Germany and Adolf Hitler, Germany's leader, or Führer. Since coming to power in 1933, Hitler and the Nazis wasted no time in consolidating control, silencing their opponents, and beginning the campaign to reestablish Germany as a dominant world power. A central part of Hitler's plan was to marginalize Jews, to make us "the other." He blamed Jews for Germany's problems, past and present, from its defeat in the Great War to its economic depression.

When Germany annexed Austria in March of 1938 and occupied the Sudentenland area of Czechoslovakia six months later, discrimination against Jews increased there as well. New restrictions made life for Jews in these areas more and more precarious.

Before we had a chance to absorb all that news, we were hit by even worse; on Hitler's orders, thousands of Polish Jews, perhaps as many as 17,000, had been expelled from Germany. The Nazi government had told them they were no longer welcome, that they were unworthy to live on German soil. The Polish government was intent on proving that it was as antisemitic as the Nazis and so refused to grant the refugees permission to reenter their homeland. Reports reached us that these Polish Jews were languishing on the border in a squalid no-man's-land of temporary camps. Eventually some of them were able to bribe guards, cross the border, and make their way to Kraków and other towns.

In front of me, my parents still downplayed

the seriousness of events. "We've had pogroms before in the east," my father said with seeming nonchalance. "Now there's trouble in the west. But things will settle down. You'll see." I don't know if that was what he really thought or if he was trying to convince himself and my mother as much as me. After all, where could we go? What could we do?

Then came the worst news yet: In Germany and Austria, on the night of November 9–10, 1938, synagogues and Torah scrolls were burned and Jewish property destroyed. Jews were randomly beaten and close to one hundred were murdered. It seemed unbelievable to me that people would stand by while such awful things were happening. Nazi propaganda portrayed the events of that night as a spontaneous demonstration against Jews as retaliation for the killing of a German diplomat in Paris by a young Jew named Herschel Grynszpan. We learned all too soon that had been just the excuse the Nazis needed. They used this event to launch a night of organized violence across the country. Later this night would be referred to as *Kristallnacht*, the Night of Broken Glass, because of the thousands of windows that had been shattered in synagogues, in Jewish homes and businesses. In fact, much more than glass was shattered that night.

It had been our fervent hope that somehow the Nazis would come to their senses and the persecution would stop. Even though my father tried to reassure me that we were safe and that the situation would calm down, for the first time, I was really scared.

The possibility of war grew stronger. I heard talk of it in school, on the streets, everywhere I went. The news reported that Polish government officials had gone to Germany to meet with that country's leadership to try to avert war. No matter how much my parents wanted to shield me, there was no way of protecting me from the growing fear that soon we would be at war with Germany.

One time I went to the main square in Kraków to hear a speech by a famous Polish general, whose name I no longer remember. He stood proudly, extravagantly praising our nation's army. He touted their bravery and vowed that if war came, Polish soldiers would not give the Germans who dared to invade so much "as a button from their uniforms." All of us wanted to believe the bravery of our soldiers could somehow defeat the mighty German military with all its planes and tanks. I'm sure my parents and many others had their doubts, but nobody wanted to appear unpatriotic or contribute to the alarm.

During the summer of 1939, all of Kraków began to prepare for war in earnest. We boarded up the windows of our ground-floor apartment, and I helped my parents tape Xs across the windowpanes to prevent the glass from shattering. We tried to stock up on a few extra tins of food. Some families hurried to remodel their cellars into bomb shelters. I began to feel more nervous excitement than fear during all the preparations and the making of emergency plans. Unlike my parents, I had no concept of what war was actually like.

In this tumultuous time I grew ever closer to my brother Tsalig. A self-taught electrician, Tsalig was in high demand to install electricity in our neighbors' newly reconfigured cellars. I think he knew I needed the comfort of his presence because he sometimes let me go along with him and carry his tools. More and more, I tried to model myself after him, and I was pleased whenever anyone looked at the two of us and commented on how much we looked and even walked alike. When we lined up our shoes at bedtime, I could see from the way they curled up at the toes that we really did walk the same way.

Some Jews prepared for war by leaving Kraków. They reasoned that eastern Poland, closer to the Soviets, would be safer than the west, with its proximity to Germany. One Jewish family in our building took a barge up the Vistula River to Warsaw, more than one hundred fifty miles to the northeast. Before they left, the man of the family entrusted my father with the key to their apartment, never doubting that he and his family would soon return to reclaim it. We never saw them again.

As the days grew increasingly tense, my mother clearly missed more and more her village and the support of her extended family. After all, in order to join her husband, she had left her parents, aunts, uncles, cousins, and in-laws in Narewka. She had met and made friends with a few other women married to men who worked in the same factory as my father, but having acquaintances was not the same as having her family. I loved city life; but for my mother, the adjustment was very difficult. She just wanted to go home. However, without my father's consent and blessing, she would never consider leaving. And my father couldn't imagine abandoning the life in Kraków he had worked so hard to construct for himself and his family.

Then, in the predawn hours of September 1, 1939, an air-raid siren jolted me out of sleep. I ran from the bed to the other room and found my parents already there, listening intently to the radio. In somber tones a newscaster reported the sketchy details that were available. German tanks had crossed the border into Poland; the Luftwaffe, the German air force, had attacked a Polish border town, and the invasion of Poland by the Germans had begun.

As the air-raid sirens blared, my parents, Tsalig, Pesza, David, and I hurried single file down the stairs to the cellar, where we joined our neighbors. Within minutes, we heard planes flying overhead. We expected the sounds of exploding bombs to follow, but strangely, they didn't. When the all-clear signal began to wail, we went back upstairs to our apartment. I peeked out the window and heaved a sigh of relief when there were no German soldiers in sight. Only an eerie quiet filled the streets. When we learned two days later that France and England had declared war against Germany, I felt hopeful. Surely they would quickly come to our defense, I thought. But in the days that followed, no help came.

The Polish army, no matter its bravery, proved unable to stop the flood of German soldiers who had crossed into Poland and quickly moved east.

There was a complete collapse, ending the life we had known in Kraków.

In the first days after the outbreak of war, many adult males—both Jews and non-Jews—fled east, away from the front. Based on their experiences in the Great War, people assumed women and children would be safe, but able-bodied men would be conscripted into the German army as forced laborers. Since my father and Hershel were the most likely ones to be taken, they decided to join the exodus and head back to Narewka. Because the journey would be perilous as the Germans advanced and because Tsalig, David, and I were still young enough, or looked young enough, to be spared, we were to stay in Kraków with our mother. One morning in a frenzy, Father and Hershel dressed quickly, gathered a little food, and, without extended good-byes, left. There were tears, but only from those of us who remained behind. I remember staring at the door as it closed, wondering when or if I would ever see my father and brother again.

Five days after that first air-raid siren, we heard a

rumor that there were guards on the bridges of the Vistula River. My spirits lifted. Surely they must be French or English soldiers coming to our rescue! They would stop the Germans, and my father and Hershel would be able to return. Without asking my mother's permission, since she surely would not have given it, I sneaked out of our apartment to take a look for myself. I wanted to be the one to bring my family the good news that we were no longer in danger and would soon be reunited.

In the foreboding silence, I followed my usual path to the river. Where was everyone? Why weren't people out cheering and celebrating the soldiers who had come to our defense? As I neared the Powstancow Bridge and the soldiers came into focus, I slowed my pace. My heart sank. From the symbols on their helmets, I knew the soldiers weren't French or English. They were German. It was September 6, 1939. Less than a week after crossing the border into Poland, the Germans were in Kraków. Although we didn't know it then, our years in hell had begun.

THREE

A BEDRAGGLED FIGURE slowly made his way up the front steps of our building and appeared at our apartment door. I didn't recognize him until he entered our apartment and collapsed into a chair. That was how much my father had changed in the course of the few weeks he had been gone. My mother, sister, brothers, and I embraced him, but our happiness lasted only a moment. It was followed by fear about what might have happened to Hershel. My father assured us that Hershel was safe, although I suspect he had doubts that he shared secretly with my mother. Father recounted that he and Hershel had joined a crowded trail of refugees heading north and east. Determined to stay ahead of the German tanks and troops, they had walked with the others fleeing the invading soldiers, from dawn to night, sleeping a few hours in fields where they found their only food, ears of corn plucked right off the stalks and eaten raw. Whenever they approached a town, a rumor would sweep through their ranks that the Germans were already there. With alarming speed, the Germans had taken over all of western Poland and were pushing east.

Hershel was young and strong and could travel faster than my father. At the same time, my father was rethinking his impulse to leave his wife and children. So they decided that Hershel would continue alone to Narewka, and my father would return to Kraków and take his chances with the occupying army. The travel was hazardous and slow, but he finally succeeded in reaching home. I was thrilled to have my father back with us.

As the Nazis tightened their grip on Kraków, Jews were barraged with all kinds of insulting caricatures. Demeaning posters appeared in both Polish and German, depicting us as grotesque, filthy creatures, with large, crooked noses. Nothing about these pictures made any sense to me. In my family we didn't have many clothes, but my mother worked hard to keep them clean and we were never dirty. I found myself studying all our noses. None was particularly big. I couldn't understand why the Germans would want to make us look like something we were not.

Restrictions rapidly multiplied. It seemed like there was almost nothing Jews were still allowed to do. We were no longer permitted to sit on park benches. Then we were banned from the parks altogether. Ropes went up inside the streetcars, designating seating for gentiles— non-Jewish Poles—in the front of the cars and for Jews in the rear. At first I found the restriction irritating. It ruined my chance to play the game of evading the conductor with my pals. Soon there would be no chance to play my game at all because Jews were prohibited from using any public transportation. Gradually the boys with whom I had shared so many adventures, who had never cared that I was Jewish, started ignoring me; then they began muttering nasty words when I was near; and finally, the cruelest of my onetime friends told me that they would never again be seen playing with a Jew.

My tenth birthday, on September 15, 1939, passed unnoticed amid the confusion and uncertainty of those first weeks of German occupation. Fortunately, Kraków was spared the destructive bombardments that targeted Warsaw and other cities; even without the threat of bombs, there was terror on the streets. The German soldiers acted with impunity. One could never predict what they would do next. They looted Jewish businesses. They evicted Jews from their apartments and moved in, confiscating their belongings. Orthodox Jewish men were special targets. Soldiers would grab them off the street, beat them, and cut off their beards and side curls, known as *payot*, just for sport, or what they considered sport. There were some gentile Poles who also saw new opportunities. One morning several Poles stormed our building to raid the apartment upstairs, where the Jewish family that fled to Warsaw had lived. They banged on our apartment door. When my father refused to give them the key that had been entrusted to him, they simply raced up the stairs, broke in, and ransacked the place anyway.

Not long after that, Nazi entrepreneurs arrived on the scene in the hope of making their fortune off the misery of Jewish factory owners who were no longer permitted to own a business. The glass factory where my father worked was one of those targets. The Nazi businessman who took over the company immediately fired all the Jewish workers, all except my father. He was spared because he spoke German. The new owner made my father the official liaison, akin to a translator, between himself and the Christian Poles still allowed to work. For the first time in months, I saw my father look a bit more confident. He insisted that the war wouldn't last long and since he had a job, we would be safe. By next year, maybe by the end of this year, he predicted, it would all be over. Just as the Germans had left at the end of the Great War, so they would leave again. I suspect that there were Jewish parents all across Kraków who delivered similar messages to their children, not only to comfort them but also to reassure themselves. My father was making the same mistake so many others were, believing that the Germans with whom he was now dealing were no different from the ones he had known before. He had no idea, nor could he have had, of the limitless inhumanity and evil of this new enemy.

One evening, without warning, two members of the Gestapo—the German secret police— burst through the front door of our apartment. The Poles who had pillaged our neighbors' apartment had tipped them off, telling them that we were Jews and that my father had refused to hand over the key. Reporting him was their chance for revenge. In front of us, these thugs, who could not have been more than eighteen years old, taunted my father, shouting at him to tell them where he had hid the key. They smashed dishes and pushed over furniture. They shoved my father up against the wall and demanded to know where we kept our money and jewels. I guess they really didn't take a close look at our modest apartment. They just followed their racist ideology that all Jews hoarded wealth. Despite their brutality, my father thought he could reason with them, that by using calm logic, he could convince them that we had no money or jewels.

"Look around," he said to them. "Do we seem rich?"

When he realized that they weren't interested in his arguments, he did something even worse. He said he would report them to their supervisors, the Nazi officials he knew at the factory. His threats only inflamed them. They beat him with their bare fists, slammed him to the floor, and choked him. I was sickened by their ruthlessness. I wanted to run away so I didn't have to watch, but I felt like my feet were rooted in concrete. I saw the shock and shame in my father's eyes as he lay helpless in front of his wife and children. The proud, ambitious man who had brought his family to Kraków for a better life was powerless to stop the Nazi brutes who dared break into his home. Suddenly, before I realized what was happening, these bullies dragged my father out of the apartment, down the stairs, and into the night.

Those were the worst moments of my life.

For years after, those scenes of horror replayed in my mind. In a way, that terrible episode became not only the precursor but also the symbol for all the horrible viciousness that would follow. Until that instant when I saw my father beaten and bloody, I had somehow felt I was safe. I know how irrational that must seem, given what I saw happening around me; but until that evening I had thought I had a special immunity, that somehow the violence wouldn't touch me. Until that instant, when I saw my father brutalized before my eyes, I knew different. The realization convinced me I couldn't be passive; I couldn't simply wait for the Germans to be defeated.

I had to act.

I had to find my father.

In the days that followed, my brother David and I searched all over Kraków, trying to find where the Gestapo had taken him. We went to every police station and government building, any place that had the Nazi flag draped outside. Because both my brother and I could speak German and because the full villainy of the Germans was not yet evident, we brazenly questioned every German we thought might know something. Only now do I realize what we did was quite simply crazy. With every German we approached, we put our lives in danger. Despite all our efforts, we came up empty. Nobody admitted to knowing that our father had been arrested, let alone where he was being held. It was the worst possible nightmare. Pesza went with David and me to a lawyer, whom we begged for help. He sent us home with the promise that he would find our father although he really had no idea where to begin.

With each dead end, I felt an escalating fear. I did my best to hide it and appear strong for my mother, but sometimes she shook me awake at night because I'd had another nightmare, reliving those awful moments when my father was beaten before my eyes. I tried to keep from thinking the obvious: If the Nazis could beat him in front of all of us, what might they do to him when he was out of our sight? When I thought of him suffering, I even began to feel a little guilty for hoping that he was still alive. I didn't want him to have to endure more beatings or to be tortured. Was there really any chance that he would ever return?

As days turned into weeks and the likelihood

of finding Father deteriorated, our situation became increasingly desperate. My father had kept a savings account in a Kraków bank, but those funds had disappeared when all Jewish bank accounts became the property of the Nazis. Now what little money we had was nearly gone. We did have a meager emergency reserve, a secret stash of ten gold coins my grandmother had given my mother before we left Narewka. One by one, my mother traded the coins for food. All too soon the coins were gone, and with them, our only safety net.

My mother was frantic, beside herself with fear and anxiety. In a city occupied by the enemy, away from the protection of family in Narewka, she nearly broke down. Nights were especially difficult, for they were the few hours when she couldn't busy herself feeding or caring for us. She tossed restlessly in the bed. I could feel her body shudder as she cried out, "What will we do? How will we live?" I felt determined to help her somehow, to relieve her anguish and to show her she could rely on me; but, as her youngest child, I doubt my reassurances gave her much confidence. She was on her own, weighted down with the staggering burden of sole responsibility for keeping her children and herself alive.

At the beginning of December 1939, the Nazis decreed Jews could no longer attend school. When I first heard of this new restriction, I felt a brief sense of freedom. What ten-year-old wouldn't enjoy a few days off from school? But the feeling didn't last long. I quickly realized the vast difference between choosing not to go to school for a day or two and being forbidden to ever attend. It was just one more way the Nazis sought to take everything of value away from us.

I now joined David and Pesza in looking for jobs. It wasn't easy, since there were lots of other Jewish kids doing exactly the same thing. David managed to find work as a plumber's helper, carrying his tools and assisting him in a number of ways. My sister worked cleaning houses. I started hanging out at a soft drink company, volunteering to put labels on the bottles. At the end of the day I received a single bottle of soda as payment. I took it home for all of us to share.

One afternoon, as I was returning from work, I spotted one of the Gestapo who had beaten my father. I was sure of it! I don't know what possessed me, but I chased after him and begged him to tell me where he had taken my father. The intimidating figure stared down at me with disdain, as if I were less than a piece of lint on his coat. Had I known better, I would have been scared for my life. But I didn't, and maybe my boldness impressed him, because he told me my father was at St. Michael's prison. I raced to find David, and together we sprinted into the central city to the forbidding building. Sure enough, the authorities confirmed that our father was there. Though we weren't permitted to see him, just knowing he was alive gave us a renewed sense of purpose. Somehow he had held on, and so could we. David and I spent most of our days going to the prison, taking with us packages of food carefully prepared and wrapped by my mother. As I think about it now, I realize the Gestapo officer could have lied to me and I would not have known, but for some reason he didn't.

Several weeks later, for no apparent reason, my father was released from prison. The moment he came through our door was one of over-whelming relief and joy. At the same time, it brought an unexpected sadness. It was easy to see that what he had gone through had changed him. It wasn't just that he was weak and gaunt; he was changed in a more fundamental way. The Nazis had not only stripped him of his strength—although he would find a great reserve of it in the years ahead—but also of the confidence and self-esteem that had put a spring in his step. Now he spoke little and walked with downcast eyes. He had lost his job at the glass factory, and he had lost something even more precious: his dignity as a human being. It shook me to the core to see my father defeated. If he couldn't stand up to the Nazis, how could I?

As 1939 drew to an end, I realized that my father's prediction had been wrong. Our situation seemed dire in every way. All signs pointed to the war going on for a long time. The Nazis were not content with what they had already inflicted on us Jews; each day brought a new humiliation. If a German soldier approached, Jews had to get off the sidewalk until he passed by. Beginning in late November, Jews who were twelve years and older were required to wear a white armband with a blue Star of David that we had to purchase from the Jewish Council, the governing body the Nazis had appointed to deal with all Jewish matters. To be caught without the armband meant arrest and most likely torture and death.

Since I was not yet twelve, I didn't wear the armband identification; when I was old enough to wear it, I made up my mind not to. Even though my confidence had been shaken by what I had seen and experienced, there were times when I disobeyed the rules and thumbed my nose at the Nazis. In a way, I used their own stereotypes against them, since there was nothing about me that made it obvious I was a Jew. With my thick, dark hair and blue eyes, I looked like a lot of other Polish boys. Now and then, I would sit on a park bench just to prove I could do what I wanted, resisting the Nazis in my own small way. Of course, I couldn't do that when anyone who knew me was around. The friends with whom I used to play now looked the other way when I was near. I don't know if they would have betrayed me, but most likely they would have, in an attempt to obliterate their memory of how they had once been friends with a Jew. I watched them walk to school in the mornings as if nothing had changed, when for me, everything had. I was no longer the happy-go-lucky, adventurous boy who had gleefully looked forward to snatching a free ride on a streetcar. Somehow I had become an obstruction to Germany's goal of world supremacy.

My father found his own way to defy the Nazis and to help us survive at the same time, even though it meant doing something illegal. He worked on the sly, off the books, so to speak, for the glass company on Lipowa Street. One day he was sent across the street, to Lipowa Street 4, to the enamelware factory where he sometimes had repaired tools and equipment before the war. The new owner, a Nazi, needed a safe opened. My father asked no questions. He simply pulled out the correct tools and quickly cracked open the safe. It turned out to be the best thing he ever did, since, quite unexpectedly, the Nazi offered him a job.

I have often wondered what my father thought at that moment. Did he feel relief or only a different anxiety about what this Nazi would ask him to do next? He knew that whatever wages he earned would never reach his hand, but would go straight to the Nazi. In other words, accepting the offer of a job meant working for free, but it also meant the chance of protection for himself and his family. There might be someone to stand between him and the next Nazis to come to his door. It was worth a try. Refusing really wasn't an option. Maybe he sensed that there was something decent about this particular Nazi. Maybe, beaten down as he already was and ready to grab on to the thinnest lifeline of hope, he just thought, *Do as you're told. Don't make trouble. Show your value. Survive.*

Whatever his motivation, my father accepted the job on the spot. In doing so, he made a decision that had unimaginable consequences.

The Nazi businessman whose safe he cracked, who had just hired him, was Oskar Schindler.

FOUR

OSKAR SCHINDLER has been called many names: scoundrel, womanizer, war profiteer, drunk. When Schindler gave my father a job, I didn't know any of those names, and I wouldn't have cared if I had. Kraków was filled with Germans who wanted to make a profit from the war. Schindler's name meant something to me only because he had hired my father.

That fortunate encounter over the safe resulted in my father becoming one of the first Jewish workers at the company Schindler initially leased and then, in November 1939, took over from a bankrupt Jewish businessman named Abraham Bankier. In fact, of the two hundred fifty workers Schindler hired in 1940, only seven were Jews; the rest were Polish gentiles. Schindler renamed the company Deutsche Emalwarenfabrik, German Enamel Works, a name designed to appeal to German army contractors. He called it Emalia for short. Armies need a lot more than weapons and bullets to fight a war. As a clever businessman, Schindler seized the opportunity and began producing enamelware pots and pans for the Germans, a line of production guaranteed to generate a large ongoing profit, especially since his labor costs were minimal. He could exploit Polish workers at low wages and Jews for none at all.

Although my father didn't bring home any money, he was able to bring home some pieces of bread or coal in his pockets. More importantly, his job gave us something else, something that I valued more, even when I was hungry and it was hard to think about anything other than the gnawing in my stomach. Working for Schindler meant that my father was officially employed.

It meant that when he was stopped on the street by a German soldier or policeman who wanted to grab him for forced labor, to sweep the street or haul garbage or chop ice in winter, he had the necessary credential as protection. It was called a *Bescheinigung*, a document stating that my father was officially employed by a German company. It was a shield of protection and status. It didn't make him invincible to the whims of the Nazi occupiers, but it made him a lot less vulnerable than he had been when he was unemployed.

I don't know how much he knew about what my father did each day, but Schindler certainly realized he was a skilled, resourceful worker. His safecracking prowess had earned him Schindler's respect. He kept on earning that respect day after day. Schindler knew little about the nuts and bolts of manufacturing and wasn't interested in learning. He had employees to handle all that. My father worked long hours at Emalia and then put in second shifts at his old glass factory. Both were sources of small amounts of food. He also made arrangements with his gentile friend Wojek to sell a few of his fine suits on the black market. Wojek kept some of the money as payment for his efforts, but what remained was enough to provide us with a bit more to eat.

Meanwhile, in Kraków, the Germans tightened their grip on us. Jewish parents could no longer reassure children with the phrase "It will soon be over," and a new phrase surfaced: "If this is the worst that happens." My mother and father also adopted this saying as a tool of survival, perhaps as a way of keeping darker thoughts at bay. When forced to hand over our radio to the Nazis, we silently repeated the words; whenever a German was near, we whispered to ourselves, "If this is the worst . . ."

In the first months of 1940, I could still walk the streets of Kraków in relative freedom, even if no longer fearlessly. I could "pass" as a gentile because I was still young enough not to have to wear the identifying Star of David. Every day I watched the German soldiers in their field-gray uniforms who guarded a petroleum tank across the street from our apartment. I couldn't help but be intrigued by them and by the well-polished rifles they carried. After all, I was an inquisitive kid. The soldiers, really not much older than I, were cordial, even friendly. Since I spoke German, I probably seemed pretty harmless to them. Having the occasional chat with me helped break the monotony of their days. They even let me inside the guard station a few times and shared a piece of chocolate from their rations.

However, German soldiers could change in an instant from cordial to brutal. If they were bored or had had too much to drink, they might single out a traditionally dressed Jew for a beating. Powerless to stop the abuse, I felt ashamed and confused whenever I witnessed such incidents. Why did the Nazis hate us so much? I had known many men, my grandfathers included, who were traditionally dressed Jews. There was nothing demonic or unclean about them, no reason for them to be subjected to such violence, but the message on Nazi propaganda posters plastered all over the city told a different story. With their distorted, lice-infested figures and captions of hate, they made it seem permissible, even proper, to attack a Jew even if he differed from the poster portrayal.

Then one night I experienced the soldiers' wrath firsthand. Someone tipped them off that I, the very same boy who joked with them in German and whom they sometimes treated like a younger brother and allowed to hang out in their guard booth, was a Jew. As I was sleeping, they shoved their way into our apartment and grabbed me out of bed by the hair.

"What's your name?" they shouted. "Are you a Jew?"

I replied that I was. They slapped me, furious that they had assumed I was a "normal" kid. Fortunately, they didn't take the abuse beyond their slaps and abruptly left our apartment. I ran into my mother's arms, shaking and crying, and this time I was the one who thought, *If this is the worst that happens . . .*

In May 1940, the Nazis began to implement a policy to "cleanse" Kraków, the capital of the German-controlled territory called the Generalgouvernement, of its Jewish population. The Germans decreed that only 15,000 Jews would be allowed to remain in the city. Over the next months, tens of thousands of frightened Jews departed for the outlying towns and villages from which many of them had so recently fled. Most went voluntarily, glad to be able to take a few of their possessions with them and relieved to escape the constant harangues and threats of the Nazis.

My parents tried yet again to put a positive spin on this new turn of events. They told us the departing Jews were going to better lives away from the city, where they would be in less crowded conditions and not have to endure the relentless harassment from German soldiers patrolling the streets. They even said that those who had left "voluntarily" had received money for food and travel.

I wanted to believe my parents, but my brothers and sister were not so easily convinced. If moving outside the city was so advantageous, my siblings asked, why were we always so determined to remain in Kraków? My parents had no answer to that. Later my brother David told me the frightening rumors: Those deported were not being sent to the countryside, but to their deaths. I was torn between believing these rumors must be false and knowing the Nazis were capable of anything. I only had to recall the vicious attack on my father to be sure of that.

So I felt a huge sense of relief when I learned my family would be able to stay in Kraków because of my father's work and our residence permits. My father's *Bescheinigung* from Emalia covered my mother, brothers Tsalig and David, and me. Pesza, who had been able to get a job at an electrical company, now had her own work permit. Still, we knew how fragile our security was in the face of constantly changing German rules and policies. Every time German soldiers banged on our door, we flashed the permits and held our collective breath for the brief but interminable inspections.

My father's job at Emalia helped us in other ways too. He received lunch at the factory. He never ate all of it, no matter how hungry he was, and brought home whatever he could. Some days that bit of smuggled food made the difference between hunger and starvation. When the weather turned cold, my father managed to tuck a few pieces of coal from the factory furnaces in his pockets, even though it was forbidden to take anything from the factory grounds. During the long winter nights, those few pieces of coal provided our only heat as we huddled around the stove. Every Friday, without fail, my mother would light the Shabbat candles just long enough to say the evening blessings.

Because the candles were nearly impossible to find even on the black market, she blew them out immediately after the prayers. But it was enough. During those brief minutes, with the glow of the candles, I felt a connection not only to my family beside me but also to my family in Narewka, to my favorite grandfather, and to happier days. The ritual affirmed who we were despite the humiliating restrictions outside our door. We could wait this out and survive, we thought, as long as we had each other.

The next months brought no good news for those of us under Nazi occupation. The Nazis, however, loved bombarding us with their successes. Their triumphs were constantly announced on the radio, in newspapers, and even on big screens they set up to play newsreels with scenes of their victories. I remember going to the empty lot where there was one such screen and watching an endless parade of tanks and jubilant German soldiers as they rolled through the Netherlands, Belgium, Luxembourg, and France in May and June of 1940.

As 1940 came to an end, new rumors circulated. A ghetto would be built in a southern section of Kraków known as Podgórze. The area would be enclosed with high walls; the few gates would be guarded at all times by German soldiers. All the Jews remaining in the city would be forced to live in the ghetto and would not be able to leave unless given permission by the Germans. We knew that in Warsaw the Jews had already been forcibly relocated into a small area of the city, where they now lived in desperately overcrowded conditions. I tried to wrap my mind around this new possibility. How could this ever happen? It seemed impossible. All too soon the rumors became reality. I watched as twelve-foot-high walls went up, encircling an area of residential buildings not far from our apartment. The Nazis then ordered 5,000 non-Jews living within the area to move out so that 15,000 Jews—every Jew still in Kraków—could be crammed into these new quarters.

My father, ever ingenious, found a way to

trade our apartment for one a gentile friend had inside the ghetto, hoping the swap might provide better accommodations than any the Nazis would arrange. In early March 1941, we piled our belongings onto a wagon we'd scrounged for the move and said good-bye to our apartment, the last tie to our once promising life in the big city.

Unlike our first trip through Kraków over two and a half years ago, when we had ridden through the streets on the horse-drawn cart with a sense of excitement and anticipation, this time we felt only dread. As we approached the gates of the ghetto, I was seized by panic. I looked up at the high walls and saw that, with their flair for the sadistic, the Nazis, in the last few days, had topped the walls with rounded stones that resembled headstones on graves. Their implicit message was that we were moving into what would become our own cemetery. I could scarcely tear my eyes from the symbols of death that "welcomed" us. I stole a glance at Tsalig for reassurance, but he kept his gaze directed downward and wouldn't meet my eyes as we passed by the guards and through the gate.

Once inside the ghetto, we made our way to our new home, a building at Lwowska 18. We carried our few belongings up the stairs to the one-room apartment awaiting us. When we arrived, a couple, Mr. and Mrs. Luftig, met us at the door. They were two of the Jews who had been expelled from Germany and had somehow made their way to Kraków. The ghetto authorities, unaware of the exchange my father had made on the side, had assigned them to this apartment. Although my parents were unhappy about the arrangement, they didn't dare question it for fear of retaliation by those in charge. Instead, we coped, as all Jews in the ghetto tried to do. My father hung a blanket in the middle of the room, separating the six in our family from the Luftigs. While my mother and sister unpacked the few items we were able to bring with us, my brothers and I left the crowded room to familiarize ourselves with our new neighborhood and see what we could learn. We were determined to make the best of the situation. What else could we do?

A few days after we moved to the ghetto, the Nazis sealed the gates, locking us inside. Still, we thought, *If this is the worst that happens* . . . If only.

FIVE

"SOMEDAY I WILL TAKE YOU to America, where my son lives," Mr. Luftig promised me as we sat together cleaning his pipes on his side of the blanket dividing the apartment. In my first year in the ghetto, I often sat down beside Mr. Luftig. A patient and generous man in his mid-fifties, Mr. Luftig loved to tell me stories about his son's life in New York City, a fantasyland of endless opportunities, an abundance of food, and few restrictions against Jews. Once his seven or eight pipes were cleaned, Mr. Luftig proudly lined them up on a table. I stared at his collection with admiration. There were straight pipes, curved pipes, and even a pipe with a lid on it. It didn't matter that Mr. Luftig had no tobacco to put in them. The pipes symbolized an orderly and civilized world beyond the control of the Nazis.

Mrs. Luftig was a quiet, uncomplaining woman. She and my mother became friendly and sometimes shared the cooking duties. Working together in those hopeless conditions somehow lessened the despair. What went on inside our apartment was replicated thousands of times in the ghetto as we struggled to keep our lives and our dignity in the face of random killings, devastating diseases, worn-out clothing, and near starvation.

Since some 15,000 people were jammed into an area meant to house 5,000, at most, the sanitation system was deplorably inadequate. The indoor plumbing we had once taken for granted now was an unattainable luxury. Lines were long for the few outhouses, and in the winter, by the time I finished, my feet were nearly frozen. The crowding, poor nutrition, and lack of hygiene made disease rampant; from typhus to scarlet fever, from malnutrition to psychosis, illness of some kind struck nearly every family.

To Nazi eyes, we Jews were a single, detested group, the exact opposite of the blond, blue-eyed, pure "Aryans." In reality we were not their opposites at all. Plenty of Jews had blue eyes and blond hair, and many Germans and Austrians, including Adolf Hitler, had dark eyes and hair. But Nazi dogma grouped Jews as one, as the loathed enemy of the Aryans. For them, being Jewish was not about what we believed, but about our so-called race. It made no sense to me, and I even wondered how Nazis could believe such contradictions themselves. Had they taken the time to really look at us, they would have seen human beings just like themselves: some with blue eyes, some with brown. They would have seen families just like their own: sons and daughters, mothers and fathers, doctors, lawyers, teachers, craftsmen, and tailors, individuals from all walks of life.

The Nazis had forced us into impossibly crowded conditions designed to bring out the worst in people. Despite everything against us, we remained determined to show respect and decency toward one another. Retaining our humanity, cherishing our heritage, we fought the depravity of the Nazis with subtle forms of resistance. Rabbis resisted by conducting services on Jewish holy days. Doctors and nurses resisted by fighting to save the lives of the ill and injured and by bringing new life into the world. Actors and musicians resisted by creating makeshift stages in hidden courtyards and performing plays and skits and holding concerts, affirming that beauty and culture could exist even in the midst of the horrible circumstances of the ghetto.

I remember chinning myself on the top of a fence to see one such comedy show filled with gallows humor. Even when I didn't quite get the jokes, I laughed anyway because it was a way to show the Nazis they didn't control me. It also made me feel better for just a few minutes. Jews resisted the bleak surroundings by sharing their hopes and dreams and stories with one another, as Mr. Luftig did with me.

Some people resisted by falling in love. Couples courted and married; babies were born. Romances blossomed despite the oppression that surrounded us. It happened to my brother Tsalig. He fell in love with Miriam, the daughter of a brush maker, who lived with her family in an apartment building behind ours. For my seventeen-year-old brother, romance was an entirely new experience and a wonderful diversion from the ghastliness of ghetto life. For me, his romance wasn't quite such a positive, since it meant I now had to share my brother with someone else. As a result, I could get a little mean. "Her face is pretty, but I don't like her legs," I once griped to Tsalig—as if he had asked for my opinion. He could have gotten mad or defensive, but instead he just laughed and nudged me on the shoulder, saying, "One day you won't be so critical when it comes to girls." With that, he was off again to meet Miriam, to stroll hand in hand, maybe to make plans for a future life together.

During Tsalig's absences, I found ways to keep myself busy. I went to a secret Hebrew school in a rabbi's darkened apartment. I made friends with other boys my age, including Yossel and Samuel, whose father, Mr. Bircz, was a shoemaker. They lived in the apartment below ours. My friends and I played cards and explored the maze of alleyways in the area. We staged spontaneous "shows" of our own in the courtyard behind our building, and I mimicked a comedy routine with a hat teetering on my head. I suspect my imitation was pretty poor, but my friends laughed all the same.

I even taught myself (sort of) to ride a bike. A man in our building had a bike parked outside his apartment. One day he asked me to clean it for him. In exchange, he promised to let me take it for a spin. Though I had never ridden a bike, I was intrigued. After I finished scrubbing and polishing the bike, I climbed on, stretched my legs to reach the pedals, and wobbled a few feet before falling over. I got back on, and when I finally thought I had gained my balance, I pushed off on what was my boldest attempt, steering around the corner and gaining speed. I felt almost airborne, flying down the street. For those few seconds I was not a prisoner in a Nazi ghetto, trapped behind high walls, but a twelve-year-old boy like any other, relishing the mix of danger and excitement. Not even the inevitable end to my ride—when I crashed to the pavement, gashing my forehead—dampened my spirits or my enthusiasm.

Such diversions were precious few. I spent most of my time focused on the critical task of finding food. Every day I combed the sidewalks and alleys looking for a crust of bread or anything else edible in the attempt to combat my constant hunger. It's hard to believe that my family survived even the first weeks in the ghetto, given how little food we had. My mother concocted a variety of soups, all with water as the main ingredient, and my father, whose work permit allowed him to leave the ghetto to work in Schindler's factory several blocks away, tried to bring back a potato or piece of bread. I still remember standing by his side every evening as he emptied out his pockets, praying that buried in the lining might be some extra food we could share. Sometimes food was available on the black market, but one had to have something to exchange. The Nazis provided limited amounts of bread but not much else.

Mr. Bircz, the shoemaker downstairs, had dealings outside the ghetto. One day he returned from a customer with *galareta*, a Polish dish of jellied chicken feet. Although they had little enough themselves, the family shared their meal with me. Even with a special treat like that, my raging appetite didn't subside. I was hungry, really hungry, all the time. Sleep became my only relief, the only time I wasn't thinking about eating, but frequently visions of food filled my dreams.

My family had already spent our safety net of gold coins, and my father's savings had disappeared. All we had left to barter were the last of my father's suits. When we were most desperate, Father once again asked his friend Wojek, who lived outside the ghetto, to sell one on the black market. As before, after taking a cut for himself, Wojek gave us the remaining coins.

Other Jews were better off than we were. Some had come to the ghetto with money or jewelry that they could trade for food. A wealthy woman in the apartment above ours occasionally asked me to run errands for her. One day when I returned to her apartment, she took out an entire loaf of bread and cut off a thick slice for me as payment. I watched in astonishment as she liberally spread butter over the bread. It never occurred to me to eat this unexpected treasure all by myself. Instead, I took it straight to my mother. She scraped off the butter, cut the bread into thinner slices, and then spread the butter on each smaller piece. The whole family shared in this rare treat. That was a good day.

Without valuables of our own, my family's only hope to fend off starvation was work, since work meant food, maybe soup at lunchtime and sometimes a small chunk of bread to take home. Each of us contributed however we could. In return for food, Tsalig continued to repair hot plates and other electrical items. Later on, he worked in Miriam's father's small brush-making business, which produced all kinds of brushes: bottle brushes, shoe brushes, and large brushes for scrubbing. He also did piecework at home, earning a little money or food for each item he produced. Pesza worked at the electrical company outside the ghetto, and from time to time, she, too, brought back bread or a potato or two. My mother cleaned the offices of the

Jewish Council and of the Nazis who had offices inside the ghetto.

One day my father summoned the courage to ask Schindler to hire my brother David, then fourteen, to work in his factory, and Schindler agreed. Every day Father and David would leave and return together, sometimes with morsels of food or a piece of coal. Now I stood between them each evening, hoping against hope that their pockets weren't empty.

Thanks to Tsalig, who was always looking out for me, I, too, started working for the brush maker, stringing bristles through a board to make brushes for the Germans. Since I was only twelve, it might seem that I was young to be working full-time, but I didn't think of myself as a child anymore, nor did anyone else. I needed to contribute to my family's survival any way I could.

Did our family talk about the future or make contingency plans in case the situation got worse? In fact, we didn't. We couldn't think two minutes ahead when all our energy was concentrated on surviving to the next day. We stayed in the moment, determined to make it through the day unharmed. I kept up my single-minded obsession with finding food, to the point where I had no time or room in my mind for other thoughts. Our goal was staying alive long enough for the Germans to lose the war and leave defeated.

My father may have been terrified for our safety, but he kept his feelings hidden behind an impenetrable expression. He rarely spoke and some days barely acknowledged us. He would return from a long day of work, empty his pockets of whatever he had been able to get, and then collapse into bed. In contrast, Mr. Luftig remained outwardly cheerful. If we had a piece of coal burning in the oven, he would sit in front of it and warm his hands, with one of his pipes dangling from his mouth. That was his greatest pleasure, even though the pipe was empty. Sometimes my mother would break the silence and state what we were all thinking: "How will we make it through the winter?" she asked repeatedly to no one in particular. "How will we make it?" I had absolutely no idea.

At Schindler's factory, my father picked up rumors about the war from the gentile workers. He pieced together different bits of information from which he could track the movements of the German army and speculate on what the Allied forces in Europe, led by Great Britain, the United States, and the Soviet Union—no longer a partner with Germany—might be planning. Although we continued to hope the German army would soon be defeated, we couldn't begin to know what would happen next. The scraps of information we received were frequently contradictory.

In May 1942, we had our first taste of the even worse suffering to come. The Nazis announced there would be a transport from the ghetto to the countryside and encouraged us to volunteer to leave the overcrowded, unsanitary conditions for the fresh air and open spaces. Some 1,500 Jews volunteered to go, thinking that anything must be better than the squalid environment they were in. By June, however, the Nazis were past the nicety of asking for volunteers; instead, they demanded that all "nonessential" Jews, which meant mainly the elderly and those without jobs, vacate their apartments and leave on the transports. So far, my father's work papers from Schindler's factory had protected our family from deportation, but the Luftigs were not so fortunate. With little warning, they were ordered to pack their belongings and report to the main square of the ghetto. There was no time to help them prepare or even to exchange good-byes.

As the deportation proceeded, I rushed downstairs to the shoemaker's apartment to get a street-level view of what was happening. Scores of our friends and neighbors, including some of the boys with whom I had studied Hebrew and watched the makeshift comedy skits, silently walked down the main street toward the train station. I peeked over the windowsill and searched for the Luftigs. Eventually they trudged by, suitcases in hand. I meant to wave, to send them an encouraging sign, but I froze in fear when I saw the German guards marching beside them, prodding them along with their rifles. Mr. Luftig stared straight ahead, showing no emotion. Did he see me out of the corner of his eye? I couldn't tell. I could only hope. Gradually the Luftigs disappeared from sight, swallowed in a sea of thousands. I remained in my spot by the window until the last of the deportees passed by. Then, with a heavy heart, I climbed the steps to our apartment. "They're gone," I said sadly to my mother, telling her what she already knew.

"He left you this," replied my mother, handing me an old-fashioned, glass-lined thermos bottle. Then I pulled back the blanket separating our side of the room from the Luftigs' side, and I saw that he had left something else.

His exquisite pipes. A tremor ran down my

spine. Mr. Luftig had determined that whatever his destination, he wouldn't be needing his pipes. It was a disturbing omen.

A week later the Nazis had another train waiting and began to round up more Jews. Evictions, they called them, not deportations. This time the deportees didn't go quietly. Escapees from earlier deportations had furtively returned to the ghetto with stories of trains filled with people entering a camp and leaving empty, even though the population of the camp never increased. The more firsthand accounts we heard, the more we began to realize what was happening. It was terrifying. So the next time the Nazis started rounding up Jews, chaos erupted. Soldiers rampaged through the ghetto, demanding that people show the required identification and shoving anyone who couldn't into the streets teeming with fellow unfortunates.

On June 8, German soldiers burst into our building and once again forced their way into our apartment. They shouted, *"Schnell! Schnell!"*—"Fast! Fast!"—as my father shakily presented his work permit. He had gotten a *Blauschein*, a "blue sheet" or Gestapo-issued permit, added to his identification card, which we hoped would again exempt all of us from deportation. Now that Tsalig was seventeen, he needed a *Blauschein* of his own. Tragically he did not have one. If only we had had a few minutes' warning, we would have found a way to hide Tsalig. But it was too late. I felt my blood turning to ice when I realized they were going to take my brother. In a split second the soldiers pounced on him. I wanted to scream, *No!* and leap to his rescue, but I knew it would be suicide, and I knew that I would be endangering all our lives. The soldiers pinned Tsalig's arms behind his back and shoved him out the door. In the span of a minute, my beloved brother was gone.

I have replayed those minutes in my head countless times. We should have been better prepared. We should have had a hiding place and practiced to be ready for just such a situation. But the roundup happened to us as it did to so many others in the ghetto, without warning and with no time to prepare or react. The shock of Tsalig's arrest hadn't even begun to register when he was already gone. Seventy years later I can still see him in my mind's eye as the Nazis dragged him from the room.

In the film *Schindler's List*, there is a scene where Oskar Schindler rushes to the train station to save his accountant, Itzhak Stern, who had been seized in a roundup. Schindler reaches the depot barely in time to yell Stern's name and pull him off the train just as it starts to move. What the film doesn't show is another scene that Schindler told my father about afterward. As he was frantically searching the cattle cars filled with people, looking for Stern, Schindler spotted Tsalig and recognized him as his worker Moshe's son. He called out to him and told him that he would get him off the train, but Tsalig was there with his girlfriend

Miriam. Since no one in Miriam's family was working for Schindler, there was nothing he could do to save her. Tsalig told Schindler that he couldn't leave Miriam. That is the kind of young man he was. He wouldn't desert his girlfriend even when it would have secured his own safety.

In the next days we heard that the train had gone to a camp named Belżec, where rumor had it people were being gassed. I remember wondering, *How long will Tsalig be able to hold his breath in the gas chamber? Will it be long enough to survive?* All I could do was pray that somehow my dearest brother had been spared or had found a way to escape.

SIX

I HEARD A SHOT and then another. I felt a bullet whiz past my ear; it pierced the wall behind me. I quickly ducked into the alcove entrance of the nearest building, my heart racing. More shots rang out. Had I been hit? How would I know? I had once been told I might not feel it if I were shot. I only knew I was terrified. I banged on the door I was standing in front of and waited. What was going to happen next? Was the soldier reloading? Did he now have me in his sights? The door creaked open an inch. I pressed hard and pushed myself inside, begging, *"Prosze, prosze."* "Please, please."

"What were you doing out there?" the man asked gruffly as he shut the door behind me. I tried to answer, but I couldn't get the words out. I stared at my shaking hands. There was no blood on them. I felt my chest, my legs, my head. I was alive. I had not been hit after all. Tears rolled down my cheeks. "I was trying to help," I finally answered.

Earlier that evening my friend Yossel and I had carried an elderly woman on a stretcher to the ghetto infirmary, but we had made a dangerous miscalculation. We had waited too long at the infirmary with her before heading home and had stayed out past the evening curfew, the hour when all Jews had to be off the streets. To reach our apartment building, we had to round a corner by one of the ghetto gates where several guards always stood on sentry duty. As we ran as quickly as we could toward that corner, one of the guards lowered his rifle and aimed at us. Driven by instinct and fright, Yossel and I ran, splitting off in different directions, barely escaping the shots. The guard probably lost interest in us as soon as we disappeared from his view, but I wasn't ready to take another chance with my life. I spent the night with strangers, curled up on the cold floor, terrified and very much alone, glad that I had not been shot.

When I finally made it home early the next morning, my mother flung her arms around me. Most of the time my mother kept her emotions under control, but in that moment she sobbed hysterically. The thought of losing another son was just too much for her.

The transports had emptied the ghetto of many of its inhabitants, including not only the Luftigs and my brother Tsalig, but also Samuel and Yossel's father, Mr. Bircz, who had shared his family's food with me. As a result, space was no longer an issue, but other dangers escalated. Hunger overwhelmed us all. Disease spread unchecked, weakening, crippling, and killing indiscriminately. There was an overpowering sense of futility. Bribes had not protected even the wealthier people in the ghetto. Everyone had lost someone they loved.

By this time survival was mostly a matter of pure luck. What worked in one's favor one day might not the next day, or even the next hour or second. Some people still thought they were smart enough to outmaneuver the Nazis, that they could navigate through the maze and survive the war. Actually there was no sure way to make it through a world that had gone completely insane.

In late October 1942, news of another transport reached Schindler, so he kept his Jewish workers at the factory overnight instead of sending them back to the ghetto. He knew the fragile work permit was no guarantee of safety during the roundups. Pesza also spent the night at her factory, which meant my mother and I were alone in our apartment. My mother and Mrs. Bircz had devised a strategy they hoped would protect us. They decided to hide in plain sight, sweeping and cleaning the courtyard, looking busy and useful. Meanwhile, Mrs. Bircz's sons, Yossel and Samuel, and I would hide in the crawl space of a storage shed behind our building. It was a tight fit, since there were only about ten inches between the rafters and the roof.

In the morning the ghetto reverberated with sounds of the *Aktion*, the roundup: gunshots, shouts in German, doors banging, and heavy boots on the stairs. My mother and Mrs. Bircz put their plan into action. They quickly began sweeping the courtyard as if their lives depended on it, which, in fact, they did.

Yossel, Samuel, and I crawled up into our hiding place. With scarcely room to breathe, my friends and I tried to stay motionless and silent as we waited. Lying on a rafter, I could see only the floor of the shed below. All I could do was listen as screams and shots filled the air. The noise grew steadily louder as the soldiers neared our building. The German Shepherds used to ferret out people in hiding were barking ferociously. Their handlers ignored pleas for mercy and killed indiscriminately. I covered my ears, trying to block out the shrieks and moans and cries of "Please!" and "No!"

Suddenly my mother appeared in the shed. She had intended to bring us a teapot with water and then return to the courtyard; but as the Nazis approached, some sort of survival instinct clicked in. She set down the teapot and climbed into the crawl space with us. Packed tightly together, we prayed we would not be discovered. Then a horrifying realization entered our heads. We all stared down at the floor. In her rush to hide, my mother had left the teapot right below us. If the Nazis entered the shed, spotted it, and became suspicious, they would surely look up and discover our hiding place. We lay motionless for a long, long time. I closed my eyes, imagining bullets penetrating the rafters and tearing holes in me. We were such easy targets.

After several hours the screams stopped. Occasional shots rang out, but they came at longer and longer intervals. We seemed to have escaped the worst for now, but we didn't dare move. When it grew dark, we heard a man's voice in the courtyard, saying, "It's safe now. You can come out." My eyes met my mother's. She whispered a barely audible, "No." I understood immediately. It could be a trap. We would stay put.

That night a numbing chill descended on the ghetto. Yossel, Samuel, my mother, and I clung to each other in the darkness, teeth chattering. We lay awake, too frightened to sleep or give in to our need for a bathroom.

The following day the SS—an organization that began as Hitler's personal bodyguard and grew to have vast authority over the "Jewish question"—continued to patrol the ghetto. We could hear the random shots, the dogs, the screams. My mother's instinct had been correct. The *Aktion* was not over. I wasn't sure I cared anymore. I was at my end. Hunger, thirst, and fear had thoroughly depleted me. All I could do was think of that teapot of water my mother had left on the floor below. I tried to convince her that I could jump down, grab it, and bring it back up without being noticed, but she would have none of it. Shivering from cold and fear, the four of us remained in our cramped refuge until dusk. The hours seemed interminable.

Finally we heard another voice in the courtyard. "Chanah Leyson," a man called out. "I was sent by Moshe Leyson." Startled, we stirred from our half-conscious state. I searched my mother's eyes. She was unsure what to do. "Is Chanah Leyson here?" he asked again. "I work at the factory with your husband, Moshe." Reassured by twice hearing my father's name, my mother nodded to me, and finally, after almost two full days, we dropped down from the rafters. Pain shot through my legs as I landed on the floor. I grabbed the teapot and swallowed a few gulps of water before passing it on to Yossel and Samuel. Stiff and sore, the four of us emerged from our sanctuary exhausted, thankful to still be alive.

Her voice hoarse and weak, my mother called out to the man. "Here," she cried. "I am Chanah Leyson." She and the man spoke together quietly as my friends and I nervously surveyed the deserted courtyard. Were we really safe? Were we the only ones still alive?

Without a word, Yossel and Samuel dashed inside our building to search for their mother. Their apartment was empty; their mother was nowhere to be found. She had been seized in the roundup. Yossel and Samuel would have to rely on their own resources. They were not the only youngsters left to fend for themselves in the ghetto. Of course, adults helped them in many ways, but basically the boys knew that drawing as little attention to themselves as possible was their best chance of survival.

In the late evening, my father, David, and Pesza returned to our apartment with scraps of bread in their pockets. I tore into the food even before I hugged them, but forced myself to stop so that we could all share the meager morsels. My father delivered the latest news. He, David, and Pesza had been ordered to report immediately to the Płaszów labor camp, about two and a half miles from the ghetto. For the first time since our family had been forced into the ghetto some eighteen months before, the five of us still together were to be separated.

As the population of the ghetto continued to diminish, officials began to reorganize those of us remaining. In December, my mother and I were transferred from Ghetto B, the section where we had been living, to Ghetto A, the area now designated for workers. A barbed-wire fence went up, dividing the two sections of the ghetto. Then the relocation began. We were ordered to take only what we could carry and find a living space for ourselves in Ghetto A.

Without a moment's hesitation, I grabbed the precious parting gift that Mr. Luftig had given me, his thermos. I also carried a jacket and a blanket. It broke my heart to leave behind Mr. Luftig's treasured pipes. Before we left our apartment, my mother had me help her drag out the pieces of our furniture we hadn't used as fuel to the balcony and push them over the railing. The cabinet, table, and chairs splintered to pieces as they crashed to the concrete courtyard. My mother had decided she wasn't going to leave anything valuable or useful to the enemy if she could help it. Once again I was impressed by my mother's cleverness and courage. It felt so good to do something against the Germans, even if the only thing we could do was destroy our own possessions.

My mother waited until the very last minute to cross over to Ghetto A, rushing back to our building one last time for a cooking pot, which she wrapped in a sheet. I could hardly believe that she would take such a risk for a mere pot, but going back for it gave her one more moment to survey her kitchen and what had been our home.

Initially, we found no place to stay in Ghetto A. Door after door closed in advance of our arrival. Every apartment was filled to capacity. Eventually we found two spots in an attic. We squeezed into a space with other relocated workers from Ghetto B, sleeping in rows on the floor. My mother and I shared a single blanket.

Our situation now made our room with the Luftigs seem like a mansion by comparison.

Somehow, in these terrible circumstances, my mother and I found the will to persevere. We had to keep going for each other. Each morning my mother went to her cleaning job, and I went to the brush factory. When we said good-bye, I wondered if it might be for the last time. Every time I returned from work and found her there waiting, I felt there was still hope. Each night we prayed that my father, David, and Pesza were safe, that Hershel and our extended family were still secure in Narewka, and that Tsalig had somehow escaped and found a safe hiding place.

Then, in March 1943, the Nazis liquidated the entire ghetto. All of us remaining were to be sent to Płaszów. At least, that was the rumor. Honestly, I was glad to be leaving, thinking that once again the five of us would be together. I had no concept of what Płaszów was. I felt a naïve confidence that because I had a real job, I was protected. On the day we were to be transferred, the Germans ordered us to line up in groups according to our work assignments. My mother stood with the cleaning women; I stood with my group from the brush factory. I saw my mother pass through the gates without incident; when my turn came, a guard yanked me out of line. He clearly thought I was too young and too puny to be useful. "You'll go later," he said, pointing me toward a group of other children gathered off to the side, out of the formations. My work permit was useless.

I found my friends Yossel and Samuel already there. In the chaos of our move to Ghetto A, I had lost track of them. They had managed to survive on their own without their parents, but now we were all caught in limbo. They whispered to me, "We're going to hide like we did before. You should come with us."

I thought about going with them and returning to our narrow hiding place in the rafters of the shed, but something stopped me. I'm not sure why I felt the pull so strongly, but I knew I had to be with my mother. She and I had been through so much together. She was my strength and I was hers. So I told Yossel and Samuel, "I'm going to try something else."

I spotted another group of workers and attempted to blend into their ranks. Once again we inched toward the gate of the ghetto. And once again, as I came close, the same guard spotted me and pulled me out, shoving me away from the departing group. Although I knew it was risky, I loitered as close to the gates as possible, waiting for a moment when I might be able to dart through them. At long last, the guard was called away. I saw my chance and joined another group. With a lump in my throat, I moved forward, closer and closer to the exit, desperately hoping the guard would not reappear. As I reached the gate, two officers waved me through, and I was now among those headed to Płaszów. My heart was racing. All I wanted was to see my family again, no matter what the situation.

As I walked out of the ghetto with its tombstone-crowned walls and along the streets of Kraków, I was dumbfounded to see that life seemed just as it had been before I entered the ghetto. It was as if I were in a time warp . . . or as if the ghetto were on another planet. I stared at the clean, well-dressed people, busily moving from place to place. They seemed so normal, so happy. Had they not known what we had been suffering just a few blocks away? How could they *not* have known? How could they not have done something to help us? A streetcar stopped, and passengers boarded, oblivious to our presence. They showed absolutely no interest in who we were, where we were going, or why. That our misery, confinement, and pain were irrelevant to their lives was simply incomprehensible.

As we neared the Płaszów camp a short while later, I was still overjoyed I had succeeded in leaving the ghetto. All that mattered to me was that I would be with my family again. As I entered the chaos of Płaszów, I saw before me a world far worse than I ever could have imagined, far worse than I ever thought possible. Stepping through those gates was like arriving at the innermost circle of hell.

SEVEN

MY FIRST IMPRESSION of Płaszów as hell on earth never changed. I only needed one look to see that this was an entirely foreign place. No matter how difficult life had been in the ghetto, at least outwardly it had appeared a familiar world. Yes, we were packed like sardines into too few rooms, but those rooms were in normal apartment buildings. There were streets and sidewalks and the sounds of a city beyond the walls.

Płaszów was an alien world. It was built on two Jewish cemeteries that the Nazis had desecrated and destroyed. It was barren, dismal, chaotic. Rocks, dirt, barbed wire, ferocious dogs, menacing guards, and acre after acre of drab barracks stretched as far as I could see. Hundreds of prisoners in threadbare clothing hurried from one work detail to another, threatened by gun-wielding German and Ukrainian guards. The moment I entered the gates of Płaszów, I was convinced I would never leave alive.

Immediately, the guards divided our group by gender. I shuffled into my assigned barracks on the men's side of the camp. My hope of finding my family plummeted when I learned that I was to stay there indefinitely. I had no idea where my father and David might be. With only my precious thermos bottle, my legacy from Mr. Luftig, and my blanket, I crawled onto a narrow wood shelf and lay down. Famished but with no prospect of food, in a cramped room filled with strangers, mercifully, I quickly sank into the oblivion of sleep.

All too soon lights flashed on. Although it was still pitch-black outside, guards beat with their sticks on the bunks and shouted at us, *"Steh auf! Steh auf!"* "Get up! Get up!" It was time to assemble for work assignments. Half asleep, I got down from the shelf and joined my group along with row upon row of prisoners from the other barracks. We stood in the dark and cold for hours; we were counted, counted again, randomly abused—verbally, physically, or both—threatened, counted again, and finally assigned to work. The work was both menial and dangerous. Most days I hauled lumber, rocks, and dirt to build more barracks. At the end of the day we received a pitiful portion of watery soup. Then I returned to my shelf in the barracks for a few hours of restless sleep before beginning the ordeal all over again the next morning.

The room where we slept was so crowded that if I left to use the latrine, I would lose my spot. When I returned I had to elbow my way back into my space. One night as I stumbled back into my bunk, I found my blanket was gone. I had stupidly left it there, and another prisoner, perhaps even colder and more desperate than I, had taken it. I was left to wrap my arms around myself, think of my mother's embrace, and will myself to sleep.

Then the miraculous happened. Some of the men who had begun to watch out for me told me where the Schindler Jews had been assigned. I resolved to search until I found my father and David. This was not an easy decision. I had to be alert every second. If I were spotted, I could be killed; but my yearning to see my father and brother overpowered reason. Weak as I was, I stole away, determined to find my father and brother. Finally, totally exhausted, when I thought I would have to abandon my search, I opened one more door.

There they were.

I had never thought of my father and brother as beautiful, but right then I thought they were the most beautiful people I had ever seen.

When they recognized me, they were as excited as I was, hardly daring to believe that I had made it out of the ghetto. "We thought you had been deported," David said. As he spoke, I saw pain and helplessness in my father's eyes as he realized how weak and emaciated I had become. We talked in whispers for a few nervous minutes. As I left, my father promised that he would ask Schindler to hire me. Meanwhile, he cautioned, I must stay where I had been assigned and avoid attracting any attention.

A week or so later, I had learned enough about the layout of the camp to guess where my mother was. Płaszów was frequently chaotic as construction continued and new prisoners arrived daily. One afternoon I took advantage of the pandemonium to sneak into the women's section to find my mother. I was so small and thin, and my hair was so shaggy, I could pass for a girl; I knew I would be severely punished if I were discovered. Yet the danger was worth it if I could find my mother. I admit on that day I was just plain lucky. Without too many wrong turns, I found her barracks. She was lying on her wooden shelf. When she saw me, she couldn't believe her eyes; to my disappointment, she seemed more startled than happy.

"How did you get here?" she asked. Before I could answer and tell her that I had found my father and brother, she told me, "You can't stay. You have to go." She could not hold back the tears as she uttered the words that would send me away from her. At the very last moment she reached into the pile of rags on the shelf where she slept and pulled out a walnut-size piece of dry bread. It was all in the world my mother had to give me, the best she could do. I'm sure it was the only food she had. She embraced me for a few priceless seconds, pressed the bread into my hand, and pushed me out the door. It broke my heart to leave her, and it broke hers to send me away.

If I had known at that moment I would not see her again all that year, I probably wouldn't have left her. Had I stayed, both of us, and perhaps others in her barracks, could have paid with our lives.

It was terrible to be alone without my parents, not knowing where Tsalig and Hershel were, or even if they were still alive. Especially at night I tried to remember their faces. I told myself they were thinking of me even as I was thinking of them; in our minds and hearts we were together. But that thought wasn't enough to comfort or sustain me. All I could do was hold on and hope that my father would somehow find a way for me to be with him. Meanwhile, I did as I was told. Some days I hauled lumber or stones; other times I pounded rocks into gravel or dug up cemetery markers that the Nazis then used to pave the roads. It was exhausting, hazardous work, and a single misstep could mean death.

One day, while carrying a large rock, I slipped on a broken headstone and badly gashed my leg. I had to go to the camp infirmary to have the cut bandaged. I learned later the commandant of Płaszów, SS Hauptsturmführer Amon Goeth, had entered the infirmary shortly after I had left and shot all the patients, just shot every single one of them for no reason except that he felt like it. Had I remained just a few minutes longer, I would have been executed with the others. When I heard what had happened, I promised myself no matter what, I would never go to the infirmary again.

Avoiding the infirmary didn't mean escaping the net of cruelty Amon Goeth cast over the camp. When my work detail passed men in other groups, I would hear the whispers being exchanged as they kept tally of the casualties by Goeth and his henchmen as if they were soccer scores.

"What's the total today?" someone might ask. "Jews twelve, Nazis zero." It was always a zero for the Nazi dead.

As the winter of 1943 began, Goeth's wrath intensified. I had been ordered to shovel snow with a group of men. With no winter clothes, I was so frozen, I could hardly hold the shovel. Suddenly Hauptsturmführer Goeth showed up and on a whim demanded that the guards lash each of us twenty-five times with their savage leather whips. None of us could figure out the provocation, but that did not matter. As commandant, Goeth could do whatever he wanted, with or without a reason. He seemed to thrive on inflicting agony on the helpless. He watched the spectacle for a while, then decided that the whippings were going too slow, so he had guards set up long tables and lined us up in rows, four across. With three men twice my age and stature, I went up to receive my punishment. The whips had little ball bearings at the end, intensifying the pain and damage. We were ordered to count the lashes as we were whipped. If we were overcome by the pain and missed a number, the guards started over at number one.

I leaned over the table and awaited the first lash. When it came, it felt like someone was cutting me open with a knife. "One," I cried out as the whip cracked. My instinctive reaction was to cover my backside before the next stroke could hit, so the second crack of the whip fell across my hands. "Two," I managed to get out. "Three. Four." Although I was numb from the cold, the pain seared through me each time, like being branded by a poker.

"Twelve, thirteen, fourteen." Would this torture never end? I knew I had to hold on and not falter or it would start all over again. I knew I couldn't survive another round. After twenty-five blows I staggered away, delirious with pain. Somehow I managed to stumble back with the others to our work detail. My legs and buttocks throbbed. They were black and blue for months and sitting was torture.

Driven by pain and desolation, that evening I risked additional beatings or worse by sneaking over to my father's barracks. I simply had to see him and tell him what had happened. Before I could get the words out, I began to cry. Trying to hold it together, not yet fifteen years old, I had finally cracked. I desperately needed his sympathy, but he offered none. He showed not a flicker of emotion when I arrived or when I finally blurted out my story. Instead, he remained silent, his face hardened and his jaw clenched. Perhaps what he felt was relief that no matter how bad it had been for me, I had survived Goeth's brutality. Maybe his anger and sadness were so great that he feared breaking down if he tried to console me. Whatever he felt, he didn't share it. Forlorn, feeling totally abandoned, I returned to my barracks. As I lay on my shelf, I listened as the men reviewed the day's score: Jews 20, Nazis 0. Despondently, I picked a few lice off my sweater but gave up trying to get them all. I just didn't care. The lice crawled through my hair and my clothes as I finally drifted off to sleep.

The horrific days came to follow a routine. We were stunned awake before dawn by the sound of crashing doors and shouted orders. We assembled in groups according to our barracks' number and were counted and recounted while short-tempered, cruel guards harassed us. Then we were assigned to groups for the day's labor. Sometimes we left camp to chop ice, shovel snow, or work on roads. We never got anything to eat until the workday ended. Then a big pot was brought out as we raced to retrieve our indispensable spoons and bowls. That one meal never varied: hot water with a little salt or pepper, and if we were lucky, bits of potato skin and slivers of other vegetables. The men ladling the soup were prisoners too, and sometimes one of them would take pity on me, stir the bottom of the pot, and put a real piece of potato into my bowl. That made the day exceptional. After the meal we lay on our shelves, trying to gather strength for the next day.

Through the barbed-wire fences surrounding the camp, I could look out and sometimes see the children of the German officers strutting back and forth, wearing their Hitler Youth uniforms and singing songs praising the Führer, Adolf Hitler. They were so exuberant, so full of life, while just a few yards away from them I was exhausted and depressed, struggling to survive another day. Only the thickness of the barbed wire separated my life in hell from their lives of freedom, but we might as well have been on separate planets. I couldn't begin to understand the injustice of it all.

As the months dragged on, I despaired. I didn't dare risk trying to see my father or mother again, not because I feared for myself, but because I feared the punishment that would come to them if I were discovered in their barracks. My first reaction to Płaszów, that I would never leave alive, was reinforced every day. Any day, I thought, my luck would run out and I'd be killed, either by Goeth or by one of his accomplices. I'd be a number in that day's score. Goeth was a stout man with an arrogant sneer and a bully's swagger. His chilling stare haunted me and filled not only my waking hours but my nightmares. Even when he was nowhere in sight, I felt his eyes on me.

During the day from time to time, I would see my brother or father at a distance, heading from one job to another, and the brief sighting would give me a sliver of hope. All too soon that hope would drain away.

Although Schindler had not hired me, I did have a bit of good luck. The brush factory where I had worked in the ghetto had been relocated to Płaszów, and I was assigned to the twelve-hour night shift. I was relieved to have a steady job and an official place to go. Being idle or waiting for random work assignments only invited trouble.

Working in the brush factory also meant I could be inside, where it was warmer, instead of outside chopping ice or shoveling snow. Yet the brush factory too had its horrors. One time while I was at work, a guard singled me out. I had been promoted from gluing on the bristles to fastening the wooden halves of a brush together with brads. It was meticulous and demanding work, but I had a knack for it. The guard watched me work and then pointed a gun at my head. "If the next brad is crooked, I'll shoot you," he said. I didn't pause or look up. I just kept working and fastened the halves together with the brad. Cautiously I moved the finished product toward him to inspect. It was straight. He walked away, and I continued working as if nothing had happened. Somehow, I don't know how, I kept my emotions under control.

A few nights later Amon Goeth stomped into the factory with his two dogs, Ralf and Rolf, and a squad of his flunkies. Bored and probably drunk, he pulled his pistol out of its holster and shot our foreman—simply shot him, at point-blank range, for absolutely no reason. As the foreman crumpled to the floor, blood pooling under his head, Goeth turned his attention to us.

Waving the gun, he yelled an order at his men, who divided us into two groups. Somehow I knew this separation was not a good thing. Sure enough, I found myself on the wrong side once again, assigned to a group of children and older workers. In other words, assigned to the group deemed expendable. Goeth and his men marched back and forth, debating something, I couldn't hear what. When their backs were turned, I held my breath and sneaked over to the other group, the one made up of stronger workers. If Goeth had seen me, he surely would have shot me or ended my life in an even worse way. Soon it didn't matter which group I was in. After a few minutes, Goeth lost interest. He holstered his gun, and as abruptly as he had entered the factory, he left, his two dogs trailing him out the door. We stood in our groups for another half an hour, too terrified to move. Finally one of the guards told us to go to our barracks. Once there, many of the men broke down, sobbing, realizing how close we had come to death. This time I didn't cry. I had grown numb to what might happen to me, to whatever my fate might be.

In late 1943, Schindler cajoled and bribed Goeth and other SS leaders for permission to build a sub-camp on the property adjacent to Emalia. He argued that it would be far more efficient if workers were a few steps from the factory instead of wasting precious time marching the two and a half miles between Emalia and the camp. The hours lost in forming lines and walking back and forth between the factory and Płaszów could be better spent producing goods and making a profit. The Schindler sub-camp was built, and in the spring of 1944, my father and David moved there. I learned through the camp network that Pesza had also been assigned to a similar sub-camp on the property of the electrical factory where she worked. My mother and I were alone once again, as we had been in the ghetto, but this was much worse— partly because I was separated from her, partly because this was such a terrible, dangerous place. I sank into deeper despair.

When word passed through the camp that Schindler planned to add thirty Jews to his workforce, I didn't think anything about it. However, a few days later I learned that a list had been created, and my name was on it, along with my mother's. I couldn't believe it. It seemed too good to be true. After a year of trying, had my father finally succeeded in getting us into Schindler's factory?

I counted off the days until we were to leave. Finally able to see a way out of the Płaszów inferno, I felt stronger in spirit if not in body. Luckily, my spirit willed my body to keep on going. The day before our scheduled transfer came a crushing blow. My supervisor at the brush factory told me my name had been crossed off the transfer list. I was to stay at my current job in Płaszów. No words can express the absolute terror I felt. Having been given a little ray of hope, the loss of it was worse than not having had it at all. I knew I wouldn't survive the next month in Płaszów, let alone the next year. I was starving. I lived in constant fear. I found myself cowering at the slightest sound or movement. What could I do? How could I go on?

The day the new "Schindler Jews" were to

leave for the sub-camp, I sneaked away from my job at the brush factory to see my mother off. It was a miracle that nobody stopped me as I walked across the camp toward the gates where those who were going to the sub-camp had assembled. I moved closer, telling myself I had to act. I couldn't let this last opportunity disappear. I had no future in Płaszów. I might as well die attempting to be with my mother. My last few steps put me in front of the German officer in charge of the transfer. My eyes were on a level with his enormous belt buckle adorned with a large Nazi swastika. I am sure this man was one of the ones who roamed the camp shooting people, either following Goeth's orders or just for his own perverse entertainment. I gulped and made my case to him in German. "I am on the list," I told him, "but somebody crossed my name off." The man didn't respond.

In an effort to strengthen my case, I said, "My mother's on the list."

What gave me the audacity to speak to him as

if he were a person capable of seeing reason, I'll never know.

As if that wasn't enough, I added, "My father and brother are already there."

I couldn't have put my life at greater risk.

I waited. Agonizing second followed agonizing second as the officer seemed to ponder what to do with me. I was lucky he thought at all and didn't just pull out his gun and shoot me, resolving in a second the dilemma presented to him by this little Jewish boy. He motioned for his assistant to bring over the list. I pointed to my crossed-out name. "That's my name right there," I told him. The officer peered down at me, grunted, and signaled for me to join the group of workers leaving for Schindler's subcamp.

For some mysterious reason, he responded as if he saw me as a regular human being who had made a reasonable request. Did he take pity on me, a boy separated from his family? Did he see one of his own children in me? Was he simply being a bureaucrat who didn't like the fact that a name had been crossed out without his official permission? There's no way of knowing. People like him could do whatever they wanted, show mercy or its opposite.

My legs quaking, I quickly made my way into the group and found my mother. She had been standing near the front, staring straight ahead as commanded, completely unaware of what was causing the delay at the back of the group. She could hardly contain her joy as I quietly appeared beside her and slid my hand into hers. We somehow managed to stand silently, scarcely breathing, not wanting to draw attention to ourselves. We waited for what seemed like an eternity until the gate opened. Finally our group started to move, and I dared to think my time in hell might at last be coming to an end.

EIGHT

ONCE AGAIN I WALKED through Kraków in a daze, this time unable to believe my good fortune. Had I *really* escaped Płaszów? Was I *really* standing beside my mother? Would we *really* be reunited with my father and brother? All these questions and a dozen others raced through my mind as our group of thirty approached the Emalia factory. I kept my head down, my eyes focused on the pavement. I was petrified that when we finally arrived at the Emalia sub-camp, Goeth would somehow be there and send me back to Płaszów. I convinced myself that if I didn't look at anyone, no would look at me, no one would notice me. I knew from experience that invisibility was the closest I could get to safety. As my mother and I walked together, I could imagine my gentile friends nearby, still going to school, still playing the streetcar game, but I did not lift my eyes even for a quick peek.

I saw Schindler's factory ahead of us. As we drew closer, I tensed and squeezed my mother's hand hard. What I saw was not the nondescript factory building it had been when my father first worked there. Encircled by an electric fence with imposing metal gates, Emalia now had a sinister look. SS guards, as frightening as the officer who had recently grunted me into the Schindler group, stood sentry at the entrance. For a few moments I feared that my life might not be any different here than in Płaszów.

But once we passed through the entrance, my spirits rose. The outside of the factory was a façade to placate the Nazis. Inside, the atmosphere was very different. As in Płaszów, men and women were housed in separate barracks, but unlike Płaszów, we were allowed to visit each other. SS guards were not permitted to enter any barracks without Schindler's permission. There was slightly better food—at midday, a bowl of real soup, perhaps a slice of vegetable, and at the end of the night shift, bread with oleo. By no means were those two scant meals enough to satisfy my hunger, but they were more than I had ever been given in Płaszów, more than I'd had at one time in nearly two years.

Soon after entering the camp, David and my father found my mother and me. We rushed to hug each other. At that moment, in my father's eyes, I saw a hint of his old pride. He had succeeded in reuniting five of us and keeping us alive, at least for now. "You'll work with David and me," he informed me with authority. I stared at my brother, whom I had glimpsed only a few times in two years. He was now sixteen and had grown to be almost as tall as my father, but his cheeks were hollow and his clothes hung loosely on his bony frame. "You'll be fine," David reassured me.

At long last, my mother and father could again talk with each other one on one. Their hushed conversations were brief but reassuring. Father shared his best news with me, too. Pesza was alive. Father had exchanged messages with her through a contact at the electrical works, but there was still nothing about Hershel or our other relatives in Narewka. Nor was there any news of Tsalig. "He could be out there," I once said to my father, my voice trailing off as the unlikelihood of this sank in. My father said nothing in reply.

I was permitted to stay in the same barracks as my father and brother. The terrible isolation and loneliness that had plagued me receded. The three of us shared a bunk, with David and me on the top and my father on the bottom. The Emalia factory operated around the clock, with mostly non-Jews working days and Schindler's Jews assigned to the night shifts. Schindler had expanded his factory beyond pots and pans to producing war material. My brother and I worked through the nights on a machine that made casings for the detonators on bombs. Our shifts were twelve hours, with no breaks for meals. At times I struggled to stay awake doing the repetitive work. If I looked like I might drift off, David nudged me and vice versa. At dawn I ate my ration of bread, returned to the barracks, and fell exhausted into my bunk.

It was on the "Jewish shift," as the night shift came to be called, that I began to know Schindler personally. I had heard plenty of stories about the wild parties he threw in his offices on the second floor of the factory, parties that went late into the night. Now, at my workstation, I could hear the laughter and music. After the festivities, Schindler still had the energy to make his rounds of the factory. When he entered our work area, I could smell his cigarettes and cologne before I saw him. Always elegantly dressed, he would meander across the room, stopping to chat with men working at different stations. He had an uncanny ability to remember names. I had grown used to the fact that to the Nazis, I was just another Jew; my name didn't matter. But Schindler was different. He clearly wanted to know who we were. He acted like he cared about us as individuals. Sometimes he paused at David's and my machine and struck up a conversation. Tall and hefty, with a booming voice, he would ask me how I was doing, how many pieces I had made that night. He stood quietly waiting for my answer. He looked me in the eye, not with the blank, unseeing stare of the Nazis, but with genuine interest and even a glint of humor. I was so small that I had to stand on an overturned wooden box to reach the controls of the machine. Schindler seemed to get a kick out of that.

I must admit his attention frightened me at first. Schindler was a Nazi, after all, and he had enormous power. When push came to shove, I reminded myself, he would side with his fellow Germans. That was to be expected. Furthermore, Schindler had our lives in his hands and could dispose of us at any moment.

Gradually I began to fear him less and actually looked forward to his visits. Never knowing when he might stop by helped keep me awake and focused. I felt proud when Schindler talked with me, although my pride was tinged with anxiety. I think Schindler in fact took a shine to me. He would point me out to visitors and say that I was an example of how hard his Jews were working. I had had enough narrow escapes by then to know that it was best not to be conspicuous, not to stand out, not to make myself a possible target. So when Schindler singled me out, I still felt uneasy. Sometimes he would even gesture toward all three of us, my father, my brother, and me, and say we were "a family of machinists." With a certain sense of pride, he would add, "experts," although I knew that was an exaggeration in my case. Then an SS officer with a skull and crossbones on his hat and a loaded pistol on his belt would come closer and watch me work. I didn't dare look up. I barely dared breathe. I knew that if I messed up, the punishment would be severe for all of us, simply because a Nazi was watching.

Weak, malnourished, and sleep-deprived, I wasn't much help to the Nazi war effort, but Schindler didn't seem to care. One evening he stopped by my workstation and observed me as I stood on my wooden box completing a casing.

"How many of those have you made tonight?" he asked.

"About twelve," I bragged. Schindler smiled and moved on, sharing a private joke with my father.

Later I learned a truly skilled worker easily would have produced twice that number.

On another occasion, as Schindler strolled across the factory floor, he caught me away from my station, watching a complicated machine as it was being redesigned to perform a different task. I was mesmerized by the intricacy of the procedure and didn't realize how long I had been neglecting my work. I froze when I smelled the familiar cologne and cigarettes, wondering what I should do. In Płaszów, I would have been shot or at least lashed for such a blatant infraction, for being "a lazy and irresponsible" Jew. Instead, Schindler walked by without saying a word. A few days later I learned that my brother and I were to be transferred to the factory's toolmaking area, which required higher skills and also meant we would be with our father. Rather than punishing me, Schindler had rewarded me for my curiosity.

Sometimes, the morning after one of his late night visits, I would go to get my rations only to discover that Schindler had left word I should receive two portions. He had to make a special effort to do this, and I was overwhelmed by his kindness. Other times he stopped by my father's workstation and put his hand on my father's shoulder. He would say, "It will be all right, Moshe." A true Nazi observing such an action, such humane treatment of a Jew, would have murdered them both without a moment's hesitation. Yet Schindler would even linger to chat with my father for a few minutes at a time. Sometimes, after he left, my father would discover a half pack of cigarettes, a valuable gift Schindler had "accidentally" left by his machine. My father traded the cigarettes for bread.

Such acts may seem insignificant given the scale of the evil in those years, but, in fact, they were anything but. Schindler dared to rebel against the law of the land, which was to torture and exterminate Jews, not to treat us as fellow human beings. To do that was to risk imprisonment in a labor or concentration camp or execution. Even referring to us by name rather than with a grunt and a curse was punishable. By treating us with respect, Schindler was resisting the Nazi racist ideology that constructed a hierarchy of humanity in which Jews were at the very bottom.

All I knew was that Schindler may have been a Nazi, and therefore by definition dangerous, but he acted in a way that no other Nazi I knew did. Though I didn't know what to make of it, I was impressed. I was also still wary of him. I had learned that human beings are frequently unpredictable.

Since the summer of 1941, when Germany broke its pact with the Soviet Union, conquered Soviet-occupied territory and invaded the Soviet Union, a German victory seemed only a matter of time, but actually time was against the Germans. They had advanced so rapidly, the famous German strategy of *Blitzkrieg*, "lightning war," that their supply lines couldn't keep up with them. They had over-estimated the speed with which they could defeat the Soviet army and underestimated the will to resist not only of the Soviet troops but also of the Soviet people. The German army wasn't prepared for the brutally cold Russian winter. With the bloody Battle of Stalingrad—in which as many as two million soldiers and civilians were killed—the tide began to turn against the Germans. When we learned of the surrender of the German Sixth Army in early February 1943, we knew a German defeat was probable.

If we could just hold on.

By the summer of 1944, reports were circulating that the war had swung in favor of the Allies, mainly the Americans and the British to the west and the Soviets in the east. We got fragments of information from time to time and pieced together that the Allies had landed at Normandy and were mounting an assault in the west. In mid-July the Soviet Red Army had reached the prewar Polish border. That meant the Soviet army was nearing Narewka or was already there. Perhaps there soon would be news of Hershel and our other family members.

When we found out German businessmen were packing their bags, leaving their factories, and fleeing Kraków with as much money and as many valuables as they could carry, we knew Germany was truly losing the war.

One might think we would have celebrated the news, but, in fact, we were apprehensive about what it could mean for us. Would the Germans decide to murder all of us before they left? This was not an unwarranted fear. Rumors reached us that Płaszów and all its sub-camps were to be liquidated and the inhabitants sent to Auschwitz, a huge Nazi concentration and death camp. The odds of leaving Auschwitz alive were almost zero.

Then the news became much more troubling. Schindler's factory would be closing, and he would start reducing his workforce. A list circulated with the names of those who were to be sent back to Płaszów. My name was on it. So were my father's and David's. *That's it,* I thought. The end. I knew I couldn't survive Płaszów again even if I was there with my father and brother. My mother was to stay at Emalia to help close the factory, but that was little comfort to her. How could she think of her good fortune when her husband and two of her sons were being sent to almost certain death? She broke into tears when my father told her we had been ordered to leave.

My father tried to keep our spirits up. "Schindler has a plan," he told us. "He's going to relocate the factory to a town in Czechoslovakia and take us with him." I just couldn't believe any of it. I didn't see any way Schindler could dismantle, move, and rebuild the entire plant. Why would he go through the complexities of transferring us when he could easily get other Jewish workers for free in his new location? Even if he wanted to take us with him, how could he possibly persuade the Nazi administrators, especially Amon Goeth, who had absolute final say over us, to go along with such a crazy scheme? I was convinced there was no way that Schindler could save us once we were back in Płaszów and under Goeth's control.

On the day we were to leave, there were about a hundred of us lined up in front of the guards who would oversee our return to Płaszów. I hid in the back of the group, as I often did, trying to be inconspicuous, particularly since I had been pretending to be years older than I actually was. Schindler showed up to see us off. Any other Nazi never would have bothered. As Schindler strolled past us in conversation with a German officer, I suddenly felt that I must do something, anything, to prevent our being sent back. I began to elbow my way forward to the front of the line, but I was too late. Schindler had already moved on. Impulsively I stepped in front of the line, within two steps of a German guard. I really had no idea what I was doing. Was I trying to get myself killed? The guard growled at me to get back in line. To be sure I did, he hit me with the butt of his rifle. Rather than hitting flesh, he knocked out of my hand the glass thermos bottle that my friend Mr. Luftig had given me as a parting gift.

The thermos crashed to the cement with a loud, explosive clang. It drew Schindler's attention immediately, and he turned around.

That was my moment. "We are being sent away," I cried. "My father and my brother and I!" Schindler immediately motioned for the guards to pull the three of us out of the line. We were ordered to return to Emalia.

Schindler not only saved our lives, he did something more. After he left us, Schindler went to find my mother in the factory. He told her that there had been a mix-up and that we were staying. My mother later told me that at first she hadn't believed him. She didn't think he even knew who she was, but it turned out he did. When I think of all his many actions as a rescuer, big and small, it is this one act that first comes to mind; I think perhaps because it demonstrates such extraordinary compassion. He knew my mother would be distraught, and he knew that only he could comfort her.

Now all four of our names appeared on the "list" of those who were to stay and help with arrangements for the transition. On that list my brother and father were numbers 287 and 289, and I was sandwiched between them at number 288. My mother was listed separately along with about three hundred other women.

As the days passed, it became clear that Schindler really did plan to move his factory to Brünnlitz, a town in the Sudetenland of the former Czechoslovakia (now the Czech Republic) near his birthplace. It took un- believable courage and ingenuity, not to mention enormous bribes, for Schindler to get the necessary approvals to disassemble lathes, punch presses, and other heavy equipment and transport all of the parts to that distant location. As the dismantling proceeded, it still felt like a fantasy to me, but my father's faith in Schindler never wavered. He even hid a few provisions in the storage cabinet of his lathe so we would have something to eat if and when we arrived.

While the machinery was being moved by train, Emalia closed and we, along with all the other Jewish workers, were sent back to Płaszów to await our turn to join Schindler. I trembled with fear as we passed through those gates of hell on earth. Heartsick, I went back to the same routine as before—up at five in the morning, stand in formation for hours, haul rocks, try to avoid drawing attention to myself, hear and see people be randomly shot. The only difference was now the Nazis' focus had shifted. The Soviet army was drawing closer, and the Germans were throwing their energy into covering their tracks. During the next week, some workers, my brother David among them, had to exhume hundreds of bodies from the mass graves where they had been thrown and burn them.

When he returned to the barracks, David was in a state of shock. He struggled to find the words to describe what he had seen. He wept as he told us that he literally had to reach down into the graves, lift out and carry the decomposing bodies to the burning pyres. We tried our best to comfort him, but we couldn't make the memory of what he had seen or the stench of death he carried on his clothes and skin go away. David was barely seventeen.

At Płaszów we briefly reunited with my sister, whose factory had also been closed. Of all of us, Pesza seemed to have held up best. She was young and strong and had been protected by her job, but the Nazi in charge of her company had taken his money, fled the area, and left his Jewish workers to their fate in Płaszów. Somehow Father dared to approach Schindler with one last request—that his much loved daughter, whom he had not seen in two years, be put on the list of workers going to Brünnlitz. Instantly Schindler agreed, and now a fifth member of my family was with us. Our luck seemed simply astonishing.

I distinctly remember the date we left Płaszów for the last time. It was October 15, 1944. My father, brother, and I were packed into a cattle car along with other male workers bound for Schindler's new factory. We were told the women would follow on a separate train. Guards sealed the doors, leaving us in darkness. We waited. My father, David, and I clutched hands. Suddenly the train lurched forward, causing us to lose our balance and pile on top of one another. Men cursed and groaned. It seemed the humiliation would never end. We recovered our balance and listened as the train picked up speed and headed west. I saw bits of light coming through the ceiling and walls. I hoped it might be a positive omen. After six years I was leaving Kraków, the city of my childhood dreams, the city that had become a nightmare, and was heading into the unknown.

NINE

GROSS-ROSEN CONCENTRATION CAMP. Only one hundred seventy-five miles northwest of Kraków, but more than a million miles from the civilized world.

October 1944.

I am naked.

My head is shaved.

I am shivering from cold and fear.

I am surrounded by total darkness.

Gradually night turns to day. I am still naked, now sprinting past stone-faced guards, trying to prove to them how fit I am.

Another day dawns.

Now I am dressed in rags. I have no idea how long I've been here.

Three days?

Three weeks?

I still don't know.

On the night we arrived from Kraków, we dragged ourselves out of the cattle cars and assembled on a vacant field. We were told to strip naked and leave our clothes where we stood. We were marched to the showers. By that time we had heard horrifying stories about showers spewing poisonous gas; but in this case, it was only icy water that dribbled out. After the shower our heads were shaved and we were sent back to the field to stand naked in the raw October night. We waited for something to happen, but nothing did. As the hours dragged by, we became colder and colder.

To find protection from the freezing night we stayed tightly packed together. I burrowed my way into the middle of the group to the warmest spot in the midst of the bodies. If I stood still for too long, I found myself on the periphery again. Everyone was trying to do what I was, so we twisted and moved constantly, a mass of humanity jostling in a never-ending quest to avoid freezing. Finding an opening, I would wriggle my way back into the middle again. Being small for my age had its advantages.

Finally the guards shoved us into a barracks. We leaned against each other like stacked chairs. There was no room to lie down. At least with all of us packed together, it was warmer. I drifted off to sleep. The next morning we woke up in a heap, tangled together every which way. Still naked, we were assembled and processed like items of cargo. At one station we were given numbers. At the next station our body hair was shaved. When I stepped in front of the prisoner who was to shave me, he just laughed and motioned me on. I was still too frail and too malnourished to have gone through puberty. I must admit I was glad to be spared that particular humiliation.

Next we had a "medical checkup," which consisted of our running in circles past Nazi inspectors. It was a matter of life and death not to stumble or collapse from exhaustion. I was terrified by the inspection. Even if I passed this test, I knew I could be singled out at any moment, judged too small to do useful work and sent to my death. Somehow I made it through without falling and joined the rest of the men in our group. Eventually we were allowed to pick a few clothes from a heap of discards. I threw on a shirt and pants several sizes too big for me, grateful to have a little protection from the cold.

None of us had any idea what our being in Gross-Rosen meant. Why were we there? How had this happened? Was this part of Schindler's plan that he had kept to himself? Was it merely temporary, or was it our last stop? Had Schindler encountered obstacles even he couldn't overcome?

None of us knew.

All of us began to think the worst.

As our time in Gross-Rosen stretched on, we seemed more and more like the walking dead.

Mysteriously, one afternoon we were herded onto another boxcar. The doors slammed shut and we were off into the night, the destination still uncertain. In the morning, when the doors were slid open, we saw that we had at last made it to Brünnlitz in the Sudetenland. We trudged from the train station to Schindler's relocated labor camp. This time the camp was to produce munitions for the war. Like other camps, it had a commandant and guards, but Schindler's presence made the critical difference. The camp consisted of a half-completed, two-story brick building. The factory was not yet ready to start producing ammunition. There weren't any bunks for us, so we slept on straw on the second floor. After Gross-Rosen, not one of us had any complaints about our accommodations.

The fact that the factory wasn't ready wasn't the biggest surprise or the worst one by far.

Once at Brünnlitz, we learned the women had not arrived from Kraków.

Their train had been diverted to Auschwitz.

When my father heard the news, the color drained from his face. I had never seen him so distressed. We were told that Schindler was already on his way to Auschwitz to get the women, but it was hard to believe that even he could pull this off.

Somehow Oskar Schindler did achieve the seemingly impossible. He handed out massive bribes to the Nazis in command of Auschwitz, all the while arguing that the women were "experts," "highly trained," and "irreplaceable." Incredibly, his efforts succeeded, and the women were loaded on a train, this one heading for Brünnlitz.

Rumors reached us that the women had been saved and would be arriving soon. On the day they were due, my heart raced as I stood at the factory window on the second floor, waiting for the women to appear. At last they filed into the camp. Like us, their heads were shaved and they were skin and bones. It was difficult to tell one from the other. Then I spied them. Mother! Pesza! I didn't care how my mother and sister looked. They were alive, and that was all that mattered. I felt a rare moment of total joy.

Pesza told us that as soon as the women arrived in Auschwitz, there was a selection by the SS officers. Those whom the Nazis judged healthy and capable of work were sent to the right; those they judged to be infirm or weak were sent to the left. At eighteen, Pesza was sent to the right with the younger, stronger women. My mother, in her early forties, was classified as useless and sent to the left, shunted to a barracks for the old and sick, the ones the Nazis didn't bother to feed, the ones destined for the gas chamber. In the midst of this misery Schindler had performed his magic. Had Schindler arrived just a little later, it would have been too late to save not only my mother but all the women in his company who had been sent to the left.

We spent the next eight months of the war at Schindler's munitions factory. Senior Nazis came through periodically and inspected our work. Even Amon Goeth came to visit his friend Schindler. Somehow Schindler succeeded in convincing the Nazis that we were useful and productive, even though during those eight months we were in the Brünnlitz camp, we produced almost no usable ammunition.

Though Schindler was doing all he could to provide for us, we barely survived. With the Germans losing the war on both fronts, food became even more scarce. Our soup thinned to almost hot water. The rations of bread were smaller. I scrounged for food every day. When I found a few potato peels, I would dry them on steam pipes running through the factory and share them with David. The terrible circumstances in which we were now existing brought the two of us closer together. We tried to care for each other, and we both looked out for our father.

I also got us a bit of food from the kitchen staff. They were political prisoners who formed the camp's underground resistance. Because they were from the city of Budzyń, near my hometown of Narewka, they spoke Yiddish with the same dialect I did. When I had the chance, I liked to hang around and talk with them, and we became friendly. They cooked the daily soup in big kettles. To wash the kettles, they swished water around inside them and then dumped it out. The workers agreed to let me collect the leftover water in a can. I set the can on a steam pipe until the water evaporated, leaving bits of solid food in the bottom. Somehow I could always be inventive when it came to getting a little extra to eat.

David and I worked in the tool and die room with our father. My skills had improved under my father's tutelage, and I could now perform the tasks of a more experienced craftsman.

Schindler kept to his usual schedule, entertaining until the early morning hours and then making his rounds in the factory. Sometimes he would ask me to come up to his office. The first time I climbed those stairs, my whole body was shaking. What could he possibly want with me? I tried and tried to think of what I had done wrong. By the time I reached Schindler's office, I was so afraid I scarcely heard him as he attempted to calm me with small talk. Then he handed me a piece of bread and I knew I would be all right. Schindler did not invite me upstairs often; but when he did, I always split the "bounty" with my father and brother.

One time, after Schindler had paused to talk to me at my workstation, he ordered the person who drew up the work schedule to transfer me to the day shift. That change probably saved my life. The day shift was far easier mentally and physically. I wonder if Schindler realized the gift he had given me. Not surprisingly, not all my fellow prisoners were pleased about this special treatment, though my father and David were genuinely happy for me.

Schindler told us about movements on the eastern front. Early in 1945, we knew that the Soviet army had liberated Auschwitz and Kraków. The more geographically knowledge-able of the prisoners sketched maps in the dirt, charting the Soviet army's advance. Their maps made the progress seem more real. It wouldn't be long, they said, before the army would reach us.

With the outcome all but decided, in those last months of the war it might have seemed that we would have felt a sense of optimism, but by spring of 1945, we were completely exhausted, totally depleted of any reserve of energy; our spirits were shattered, our bodies barely alive. My father could no longer stand at his machine for his twelve-hour shift. He had to squat down when no one was looking. David developed sores on his legs that wouldn't heal. I began to have double vision. I had to read measuring markings on my machine, and sometimes I simply couldn't; the fine lines on the instruments looked like tiny wiggly worms.

I don't know why, perhaps simply because the six years of stress and suffering had finally caught up with me, but I couldn't let go of the thought that obsessed me, that I would be shot with the last bullet of the war. I played out the nightmare over and over in my mind—the last day, the last hour, the last minute, liberation so close, then my luck would run out.

Really, my fears were not so far-fetched. It's good that I didn't know until later that in April 1945, the SS was ordered to murder all the Jewish workers at the factory, but Schindler managed to thwart the plan and get the SS officer in charge transferred out of the area before he could carry out the instructions. By that time German officers and soldiers were fleeing, doing their utmost to avoid capture by the rapidly approaching Soviet army. In the midst of the chaos Schindler again seized an opportunity to act on our behalf. He went to one of the abandoned Nazi warehouses and brought back hundreds of bolts of navy-blue cloth and hundreds of bottles of vodka.

With the danger of capture by the Soviets imminent, Schindler knew he had to flee. First, he made it clear to the guards that they would have a better chance of survival if they left on their own. They needed no further encouragement. The soldiers fled without a word, but Schindler remained. He could not bring himself to leave without saying good-bye and gathered his Jews together one last time. After so many years of constant fear, I struggled to believe what he was saying could really be true.

"You are free," he told us.

Free!

We were speechless. What was there to say? What words could possibly express the tumult of emotions we were feeling? Freedom seemed like an impossible fantasy. Before he left,

Schindler asked that we not take revenge on the people in the nearby town, since they had helped him to keep us alive. He gave each of us a bolt of cloth and a bottle of vodka, goods he knew we could barter for food, shelter, and clothes. I didn't have a chance personally to say good-bye to Schindler, but I joined with all the other workers in presenting him with a ring, made from a prisoner's gold tooth, which bore an inscription in Hebrew from the Talmud: "He who saves a life saves the world entire."

Just after midnight, Oskar Schindler sped off in his car. His goal was to reach the American lines, which he did. Had the Soviets captured him, they would have seen him only as a Nazi and would have killed him.

We waited in limbo after Schindler's departure for the arrival of the Soviets. Our guards had not hesitated to abandon their posts; we could have left, and yet we didn't. We had no news, no place to go, and no idea what would await us outside the camp. It was strangely quiet, like being in the eye of the storm. Some young people took up the weapons abandoned by the guards and performed sentry duty. Night fell with none of us knowing what our next move should be.

On May 8, 1945, the answer came. A lone Russian soldier rode up to the gates. He asked who we were; we answered we were Jews from Poland. He said we were free and told us to tear the numbers and triangles off our uniforms. As I think back to that moment, it seems like we ripped them off in unison, an affirmation of our solidarity and victory.

Despite impossible odds, we had made it. Miraculously, Oskar Schindler, this complex man of many contradictions—Nazi opportunist, schemer, courageous maverick, rescuer, hero— had saved nearly 1,200 Jews from almost certain death.

TEN

AFTER THE SOLDIER LEFT, the gates swung open. I was in shock. We all were. We had gone from years of imprisonment to freedom. I felt confused, weak, and ecstatic all at once.

Disoriented and uncertain, we continued to drift around the Brünnlitz camp for two days. I couldn't absorb the fact that we were now liberated, even as our enemies, the vanquished German soldiers, streamed past us by the hundreds. I stood and watched them, the once confident troops now dejected prisoners of the Soviets. Hour after hour, they trudged by, their heads down, their expressions sullen. Some of the Jewish workers contemplated revenge. A few grabbed the soldiers' boots and tossed their own wooden clogs at them in exchange. I didn't join in. There was no way to "even the score" with the Nazis, no matter what I did. All I wanted was to remember those hours forever, remember the sight of the once proud soldiers straggling past us in abject defeat.

Eventually the Czech authorities provided free transport by trains for those of us who decided to return to Poland. My mother longed to go all the way to Narewka to find Hershel and her family, but my father said it was still too dangerous to travel that far east. Instead, he decided that the five of us would return to Kraków. Of course, we all nurtured the secret hope that somehow Tsalig had escaped and would be there waiting for us.

This time the cattle cars had bunks and the sliding doors remained open. We could breathe in the smells of springtime and watch the passing countryside. From my spot, I surveyed the scenery and noticed few signs of the war that had decimated our lives. Trees sprouted new leaves; wildflowers were blooming. The scars from the war, which I felt so deeply, weren't visible in the passing landscape. It was almost as if these terrible years of suffering had never happened, but I only had to look at the worn and weary faces of my parents to know otherwise.

As the train rumbled eastward, I allowed myself to do something I hadn't done in years: to think about the future. For the past six years, thinking about the future had meant only thinking about how to survive the next hour, how to find the next scrap of food, how to escape the next brush with death. Now the future meant much more. I might be able to return to school. I might be able to have a home, adequate food, security. One day I might feel safe again.

The train stopped frequently to let passengers

off at points near where they had come from. Each time, passengers climbed down and quickly left, without looking back or saying good-bye. There was no reason to prolong the ordeal a moment longer. I watched my former coworkers scatter across Poland, one by one, family by family. All of us prayed that our suffering was over, that we could go back to our lives, to the families from whom we had been separated for so long.

Sadly, in Kraków, I soon realized the suffering wasn't over. My parents, David, Pesza, and I arrived still wearing our striped prison uniforms. We clutched our only possessions—the bolts of cloth and bottles of vodka that Schindler had secured for us—and walked tentatively through the city toward our old neighborhood. We were greeted by curious stares and an indifference that completely unsettled me. We found Wojek, the kind gentile who had sold my father's suits, and we connected with a former neighbor on Przemyslowa Street. He let us stay in his apartment a few nights and decided to throw a little party for my father. Over shots of vodka from one of our precious bottles, he confessed he was surprised that we had survived.

It became clear that many others in the city shared his surprise. To some, the Jews' unexpected return was not welcome. They wondered what we would expect from them. They had suffered their own hardships and losses during the war and weren't interested in ours. Some were antisemitic and had been pleased to see us out of what they considered to be their country, despite the fact that Jews had lived there for over one thousand years. Now we were back, causing them anxiety though we were simply trying to adjust to freedom and begin rebuilding our lives.

My mother found a tailor who sewed a pair of pants for me from my bolt of cloth—my first new trousers in nearly six years. His payment was the fabric remaining on the bolt. My father was able to get his old job back at the glass factory. We urgently needed a place of our own. We found lodging in a student dormitory that had become a receiving center for refugees. That's what we were now, I realized. Refugees. Outsiders, ironically, in a country where Jews had a long history. At the end of the war, of Kraków's prewar Jewish population of about 60,000, only a few thousand remained.

The dormitory housed other returning homeless as well. As in the ghetto, we divided the room into sections, using ropes with blankets draped over them. Soon there were more and more people looking for space as Jews returned to the city to search for their families and try to reclaim their homes and their prewar lives. Many of them came from Soviet-occupied areas in the east. One day my mother found a young woman and her mother sleeping in the hallway. My mother insisted that they share our space. Gradually each of the four corners filled with a different family.

That summer the backlash in Kraków against returning Jews intensified. A Jewish woman was falsely accused of kidnapping a gentile boy. Rumors circulated that emaciated Jews returning from the camps were using gentile children's blood for transfusions, a revival of the ancient accusation known as blood libel. The accusation, in the past and the present, was false and ridiculous, but it nonetheless put the city on edge. A mob gathered at one of the remaining synagogues, shouting slurs, and then came to our building to throw rocks at the windows. After an hour or so, the hoodlums left, but the violence revived old fears; once again I longed to be invisible. My father went to work every day, while the rest of us spent most of our time inside our makeshift home, afraid to venture out. Was this to be our future? Had we survived the war, the ghetto and camps, only to continue to live in dread?

On August 11, 1945, rioting broke out when a gentile boy claimed that Jews were trying to kill him. Hooligans attacked our building, again pelting the windows with rocks, pulling people from the first floor to beat them with their bare hands. We scrambled from our room to the safety of a higher floor. Elsewhere in the city, rioters looted a synagogue and burned the Torah scrolls. There were reports that Jews beaten in the streets had been hospitalized only to be beaten again. At the factory my father had been warned not to leave after work; the streets were too dangerous, so he stayed overnight, in relative safety. My mother, my siblings, and I faced a long night on our own.

The next day, after my father returned from the factory, we told him what had happened the night before. He remained silent.

"We can't stay here," David said to my father.

"If we could get back to Narewka . . . ," my mother offered. She often said this after the war. She had never felt at home in the city and certainly had no reason to alter that feeling now, but the real reason for her longing to return to Narewka was the thread of hope that at least some of our family, and especially my oldest brother, Hershel, had survived.

"We can't go back yet," responded my father. "Maybe never."

My father related his devastating news. My mother listened horror-struck as he told us what he had learned from his factory contacts originally from Narewka. Some had managed to go back to look for family. What they reported was terrifying. Following the invading German army, mobile killing squads of the SS, called Einsatzgruppen, had swept through the villages of eastern Poland with the sole purpose of murdering Jews. They reached Narewka in August 1941. There they took all the Jewish men in the village, some five hundred, to a meadow near the forest, machine-gunned them down, and buried them in a mass grave. The SS took the women and children to a nearby barn, where they were held for a day, and then they, too, were executed. In one blow, all of our extended family in Narewka, some one hundred relatives—my grandparents, aunts, uncles, cousins—had been murdered. It was beyond belief. As she thought of her parents, my mother could only whisper, "I hope they died before the Einsatzgruppen arrived."

All at once the full impact of what we had been told hit us.

We had never heard from Hershel in those six long years we had been separated. We had assumed he had made it to Narewka, which in 1939 was under Soviet control and had seemed a safer place for him than Kraków. Now we learned that Hershel had indeed made it back to Narewka, only to be taken prisoner and murdered by the SS assassins on that terrible day in August. My mother collapsed as the rest of us stood, stunned by the atrocity.

Many years later I went back to Narewka. A gentile Pole I met there spoke of how one young Jew had tried to run, but, as he said, "one of ours"—in other words, a non-Jew—spotted him and reported him to the SS, who shot him

179

immediately. As I think about my impetuous brother, I can imagine him being that young man who made a run for the forest, doing everything he possibly could to try to survive.

As the weeks passed, life did not improve. There were constant reports of recurring hostility toward Jews. Jobs were scarce and so was food. The future for us in Kraków looked bleak.

Early in 1946, David and Pesza devised a plan to go back to Czechoslovakia to see if they could settle there. I went with them across the border. After a few days, however, my mother sent word through a friend that she needed at least one of her children to be with her. As the youngest, still only sixteen, I was the obvious choice. I said good-bye to David, and Pesza took me back to Kraków. She then returned to Czechoslovakia and David. It hurt to say good-bye to my brother and sister. Amazingly, we had managed to stay together during the last years of the war. Now they were adults and eager to begin anew. My parents never would have tried to dissuade them.

A few months later my parents enlisted the help of a Zionist organization—one of the groups whose goal was to establish a Jewish national state. We hoped that they could smuggle us out of Poland. We did not consider going to British-controlled Palestine as the life there would be too arduous for my parents. After several weeks of anxiously waiting, our window of opportunity came. We paid a guard a small bribe and slipped across the border. We traveled by train through Czechoslovakia, arriving finally in Salzburg, Austria. There a United Nations relief organization assigned us to a displaced persons camp in Wetzlar, Germany, in the American occupation zone. On the one hand, it seemed strange to be in Germany, of all places; on the other, it felt good to be opening a new chapter in our lives.

Homeless, stateless, in yet another camp, we could have felt defeated, but Wetzlar was very different from the camps during the war. We had three meals a day, reliable medical care, and the protection of the US military. Pretty good. Most importantly, we could come and go as we pleased. I took every opportunity to go into town and strike up a conversation with anyone willing to talk with me. I befriended other teenagers in the camp, including a pretty Hungarian girl my age. I learned to speak fluent Hungarian just so I could talk with her. In fact, some Hungarians were so convinced that I was Hungarian that they spoke Polish when they didn't want me to understand what they were saying. Little did they know that Polish was my native language.

To my mother's delight, I put on weight, began to fill out my skeletal frame, and grew several inches. My hair came back dark and thick. I had new clothes, made by tailors in the camp who ripped apart military uniforms at the seams and refashioned them into civilian clothes. Someone even gave me a hat, a brown fedora. It became my trademark. I wore it everywhere, emulating in my own way my father's prewar flair for style.

Occasionally my new friends and I would argue about who had had it worse during the war. Some had been in labor camps, some in concentration camps, some even in the infamous Auschwitz-Birkenau death camp. Others had been in hiding in many different circumstances. We couldn't resist the urge to swap stories and exchange information, even though such conversations sometimes led to jealousy and anger. In a strange way we seemed to be vying for the worst experience. We all had been through our private hells, and we were still processing what we had experienced. None of us knew what to do with the enormous burden of our memories. Sometimes the pain of our grief would break through the surface and threaten the fragile friendships we were nurturing.

I never felt like the camp was home, but I began to get used to the life there as we waited to see which country might allow us to immigrate. There were lots of people like us, looking for a place that would take them in.

The Germans had ended my schooling shortly after I turned ten. My parents were concerned about my lack of education and what that might mean for my future. My father began looking for someone to tutor me, to help me make up at least part of what I had lost. In the nearby town he found a former German engineer who was now unemployed and had five children to feed. Three times a week for two years, I went to Dr. Neu's house to be tutored in mathematics and drafting. We began with basic arithmetic and worked our way up to the complexities of trigonometry.

Over time I came to look forward to my lessons with Dr. Neu. After my experiences with Oskar Schindler, I felt I could tell the difference between those Germans who had been true Nazis and those who had retained some humanity, even if they had joined the Nazi

Party. I found that the true believers would look down at their shoes or wind their watches when someone mentioned the war. When someone spoke of what the Jews had gone through, their stock response was "We didn't know." Dr. Neu wasn't like that. He asked me about my experiences and genuinely listened to what I told him. I was reminded of how Oskar Schindler had asked me questions and had waited for my answers. Dr. Neu didn't try to whitewash what had happened. One time, when I was telling him a story, his wife overheard us. "We didn't know," she muttered. He gave her a piercing look and said, "Don't say that." After the awkward moment passed, he urged me to continue with my story.

Through Jewish organizations, my parents connected with our few relatives in the United States. My mother's sister, Shaina, and brother Morris, who had left Narewka in the early 1900s, now lived in Los Angeles. (Uncle Karl had died shortly after arriving in the United States.)

Based on the reports they heard, they had come to believe that all their family in Poland had been murdered. They were ecstatic to learn the three of us were in a displaced persons camp. Our American relatives wrote letters and sent packages to us, packages filled with food donated by other friends from Narewka now living in the United States. Since we didn't have any money to pay Dr. Neu for my tutoring, we gave him items from our CARE packages; coffee and cigarettes, and food items from the DP camp my family would not eat, like canned ham.

In 1948, Pesza and David joined a Zionist group and left Czechoslovakia for the new state of Israel that had been founded that very year. When we received word of their plans, I wanted to go with them, but by this time my parents had decided we would go to the United States as soon as my aunt and uncle could make the arrangements. My parents reasoned that in America we could find jobs and help support my sister and brother, whose lives would not be easy in a country struggling to establish itself. Although I was now almost nineteen and longed to join my brother and sister, after all my parents had been through I couldn't refuse their plea for me to stay with them.

At last, in May 1949, after nearly three years in the displaced persons camp, we received word that our immigration request had been approved. Almost beyond belief, we really were going to the United States of America! We took the train to Bremerhaven, Germany, and then traveled on a former troopship for nine days across the Atlantic Ocean to Boston, Massachusetts. I spent all the time I could on deck, watching the ocean stretching in all directions. Something about its majesty, its vastness, brought me a peace I had not known before.

We slept in hammocks below deck and battled seasickness, although I wasn't as badly affected as some. We refugee passengers represented many nations and spoke many languages. I was awed by how many of the languages I didn't know. What we didn't speak was English, so we had identification tags on our jackets to make sure we ended up in the right place.

Uncle Morris's son, Dave Golner, who lived in Connecticut, found us as we were being processed by immigration after our ship docked at Boston Harbor. During the immigration procedures, our last name changed to Leyson. I had already abandoned Leib for the much cooler, I thought, name Leon. Dave knew only a little Yiddish and no Polish, so he did more pointing than speaking as he directed us from the port to the train station. He gave us spending money for the five-day trip to Los Angeles, California.

It felt good to ride the train this time, to sit in a passenger car, in a plush seat, not crammed in a cattle car. Probably some people would think our trip was an ordeal. We slept in our seats. There wasn't a shower for us to use. But for me, every minute of the trip was wonderful. I spent hours sitting by the window, watching the world pass by as we went from the East Coast to Chicago, then across the Midwest and through the Southwest.

Our lack of English made for some confusing moments along the way. For example, whenever we went to the dining car, all we could do was point to what someone else was eating or to a few incomprehensible words on the menu. Often we ended up with some very strange combinations. I also had no idea how the prices on the menu corresponded to the money in my pocket, so I would hand the waiter a large bill and wait to receive change. I gradually accumulated a larger and larger stack of coins. Back in my seat in the pasenger car, I would study them and try to figure out what was worth what. Of course, I could read the numbers on the coins, but that was not the same as understanding the values.

One afternoon a woman a few seats away observed me looking at the change I had just acquired from paying for lunch. She left her seat and came over to sit next to me. She smiled and took a coin out of my hand. "This is a nickel," she said. She picked out another coin. "This is a dime," she continued, "and this one's a penny." We went over the denominations a few times— one cent, five cents, ten cents, twenty-five cents. After I learned how to say the names and values, the woman smiled again and returned to her seat. She probably forgot the incident in a few days, but I never have. I still remember her kindness nearly sixty-five years later. She gave me my first English lesson.

On the train I watched as the scenery went from lush greens to dramatic reds to dry desert browns. We crossed the Continental Divide and the Mojave Desert. I thought about this new country that would now be my home. The future lay before me in a way that only a brief time before I would have thought impossible. I wasn't scared at all, even though I didn't know the language nor have a clue what I would do. I was just excited. For the first time in many years, I could daydream about the future. I knew I would learn English. I would get a job. Someday I would marry and have a family. I might even live to be an old man. Anything could happen.

As the train pulled into Union Station in Los Angeles, my mother, father, and I gathered our belongings and readied to leave. I picked up my fedora and started to put it on, but then I reconsidered. I tossed the hat back on the luggage rack and turned to leave. That hat was part of my previous life, the life I intended to leave behind. With quarters, nickels, and dimes jostling in my pocket, I stepped off the train and into the California sunshine.

I was nineteen years old, and my real life was just beginning.

EPILOGUE

IN THE UNITED STATES, I rarely spoke about my experiences during the war. It was too hard to explain to people. There didn't even seem to be a vocabulary to communicate what I had gone through. For Americans, a word like "camp" evoked happy summer memories that were nothing like what I had experienced in Płaszów and Gross-Rosen. I remember once shortly after we were settled in Los Angeles, I tried to describe to a neighbor what it was like to be starving in the ghetto. When I said we never had enough to eat, he responded, "We had rationing here, too." He had no clue of the difference between what he had experienced in having only small quantities of butter and meat during the war and what I had experienced scrounging through garbage searching for a potato peel. There really wasn't any way to talk about my experiences without seeming to belittle his, so I decided not to talk about Poland and the war. Like the hat I had left behind on the train, I tried to leave those years behind me as I began a new life. Of course, unlike leaving a hat, one cannot walk away from memories, and those memories stayed with me every day.

My parents and I focused on getting settled and finding work. We stayed with my aunt Shaina, now known as Jenny, for a few weeks before moving into a one-bedroom apartment in the building where my uncle Morris, my mother's brother, lived. My parents took the bedroom, and I set up a cot for myself in the kitchen—a definite upgrade from the crowded bunks of the concentration camps. I felt very grateful.

The three of us enrolled in English for Foreign Born classes three nights a week at Manual Arts High School. Soon my father took a job as a janitor at an elementary school. It was not the same as being the respected craftsman he had been before the war, but he did the best he could and continued to feel optimistic. At fifty-plus years, with limited English skills, he had few options. I worked on an assembly line at a factory that made shopping carts. In the beginning it was good to have repetitive tasks that didn't require speaking much English, but I knew I didn't want to spend the rest of my life doing this kind of work.

My mother had an especially difficult time learning English. Eventually she acquired enough vocabulary to be able to shop and to talk with the neighbors. She and my father joined the Narewka Benevolent Club, which had been founded by Jews who had immigrated to the United States in the early 1900s. Periodically the club would get together to sing, dance, reminisce, and raise money to help various charities. How fortunate my parents felt to be on the giving end.

My mother devoted herself to caring for my

father and making a home for us. Separated from the world in which she had grown up, she seemed to me to be lonely and adrift. Of course, she could never stop thinking about the sons she had lost, especially Tsalig, because she had stood by helpless as he had been taken away.

I learn languages easily, so it didn't take me long to feel comfortable conversing in English. With the help of Uncle Morris, I was hired as a machinist at US Electrical Motors and enrolled in classes at Los Angeles Trade-Technical College. I was learning from books what my father had learned by doing, but we worked together to master challenges of converting metric measurements to the equivalents in inches, feet, and yards. For a year and a half, I went to classes in the morning and worked in the afternoons and evenings until midnight. After getting off my shift, I would sleep in the back of the bus on my ride home. The bus driver was a kind man who would wake me just before my stop. Early the next morning I would start the routine all over again. It was hard, but I didn't think about it that way. Hard had been the grueling work in Płaszów. My schedule was tiring, but the work was worthwhile and interesting. Though I was draft age as the Korean War began, I was exempt from service as long as I was enrolled as a student.

In 1951, I finished my trade school courses, and like clockwork, even though I wasn't a US citizen, my US Army draft notice arrived in the mail. I went first to Fort Ord in Monterey, California, for basic training and then to Aberdeen, Maryland. For many young men accustomed to a civilian life with freedom and personal privacy, military life was tough and there was a lot of grumbling. I listened to their gripes and just smiled. I had a cot to myself, decent clothes, more than enough food, and I was being paid! What was there to complain about? When the drill sergeants yelled at us for not doing a better job spit-polishing our shoes, I said to myself, "Well, I won't be shot for that." I made friends with guys from places I had never heard of: Kentucky, Louisiana, North and South Dakota, and other states. When they asked me where I was from, I just told them LA. By now my English was good enough to get away with such a cocky response.

Near the end of my training, I was transferred to a base outside Atlanta, Georgia. One weekend we received passes to go into the city. After boarding the shuttle to town, I went to my favorite spot in the back to catch some shut-eye. I was startled when the driver stopped the bus and walked back to me. "You can't sit there," he said. "The back seats are for Negroes. You have to move to the front of the bus." His words hit me like a hard slap. Suddenly I flashed back to Kraków, when the Nazis ordered us Jews to the back of the bus (before they forbade us from traveling on public transportation altogether). The context was very different, but nonetheless it almost made my head explode. Why would something like this exist in America? I had mistakenly believed that such discrimination was unique to Jews suffering under Nazi oppression. Now I discovered that there was inequality and prejudice in this country that I had already come to love.

Before my overseas assignment was made, I was tested in several European languages. The United States still had many military facilities in Europe; when I earned ratings of fluent in German, Polish, and Russian, I expected to be stationed in Germany or Poland. Instead, I was given an assignment in the opposite direction... Okinawa, Japan. I spent sixteen months on Okinawa, where I served with a unit of army engineers. I supervised twenty-one Okinawans in a machine shop and rose in rank from private first class to corporal. To me that was a big deal. I treasured those two stripes on the sleeve of my US Army uniform.

When I was discharged and returned to Los Angeles, I made up my mind to continue my education. The GI Bill made that possible. I met with a counselor at Los Angeles City College, who asked me for my high school diploma. I explained that I didn't have one, that my formal education had ended just after I turned ten. He looked baffled, so I volunteered enough details to explain my past. The counselor reviewed my army experience and something clicked. He suggested that I consider becoming an industrial arts teacher. "If you maintain a C average, you can stay in school and get your degree," he asserted. I couldn't believe it. "That's all I have to do?" I asked. He assured me it was.

I ended up with much better than a C average. I graduated from LACC and transferred to Cal State Los Angeles, where I completed my bachelor's degree and earned a teaching credential. In time I earned a master's degree in education from Pepperdine University.

I started teaching at Huntington Park High School in 1959. I stayed at the school for thirty-nine years. As one decade passed into another, I put my World War II experiences even further behind me. Occasionally, when someone noticed a trace of an accent and asked me where I came from, I would reply vaguely, "From the east." I didn't clarify that I meant something other than the East Coast of the United States.

As much as I had moved on and made a life for myself, it wasn't until I met my future wife, Lis, that I felt I could truly heal. In my sixth year at Huntington Park, January 1965, she came to teach English as a Second Language and immediately caught my eye. I guess I made an impression on her, too. She had intended to stay in southern California for one semester, but I changed her mind. We spent a great deal of time together over the next months. I began to tell her about my past, stories I had told no one else since arriving in the United States. By the end of the semester we were in love. We married that summer. We moved to Fullerton, California, a few years later. We have a daughter and a son, whom we raised as normal American kids without the burden of my family's past. I did not share my childhood and teenage experiences with them until they were old enough to understand. I wanted to give our children a legacy of freedom, not a legacy of fear. Of course, I gradually shared my past with them in increments as they grew older.

My brother and sister also married and had families of their own in Israel. David has three boys and a girl and still lives in Kibbutz Gan Shmuel, famous for its orchards and its exports of fruit concentrates and tropical fish. Pesza changed her name to Aviva after she immigrated to Israel. She has three children and six grandchildren and a baby great-granddaughter. She lives in Kiryat Haim, a beautiful town on the Mediterranean, north of Haifa.

It was much harder for my parents than for me to find their way in a new country. They had survived the unimaginable, as had three of their children, but the war ripped a hole in their hearts that would never heal. There was not a day they didn't think of Hershel and Tsalig and all the family they had lost. Physically, the years of suffering had taken a toll. One time when we were in Płaszów a guard struck my mother on the side of her head with a wood plank. The blow permanently shattered her eardrum. She said that for the rest of her life she could hear her two murdered sons calling to her in that ear.

My father continued to take English classes, so determined was he to master the language. He moved from a custodial job to one in a factory as a machinist. Soon his skill as an expert craftsman became apparent, and that helped him to regain some of the pride and self-respect he had enjoyed in the years before the war. He rarely spoke about what we had gone through during World War II. He continued to be the center of my mother's world. When he died in 1971, it was fortunate that she had two grandchildren living close to her to help her through her grief. She died five years after my father.

Schindler struggled after the war. His brand of wartime wheeling and dealing was not appropriate for a businessman in peacetime. He had a series of unsuccessful business ventures and went bankrupt more than once. Near the end of his life he lived on contributions he received from Jewish organizations. To many of his fellow Germans, Schindler had been a traitor to his country, a "Jew lover." In 1974, Schindler died in humble circumstances in Hildesheim in what was then West Germany.

Up until his death Schindler kept in touch with some of his former workers. Our gratitude meant a great deal to him. He thought of us, the *Schindlerjuden*, the Schindler Jews, as the children he never had. He asked to be buried in Jerusalem. "My children are here," he once said. He is interred on Mount Zion, the only member of the Nazi Party buried there. If you visit his grave, you will see it covered with small stones and pebbles, tokens of remembrance left by those who knew him and those who didn't, but who remember the lives he saved and the courage he showed.

Now and again, I met other *Schindlerjuden* in the United States. I reconnected with Mike Tanner, who had worked on a machine near mine in Schindler's factory in Kraków. Leopold Page, who was quite a bit older than I, was devoted to Schindler and made it his life's goal to educate the world about who Schindler was and what he had done. I met Mr. Page when he came to talk with my parents about his project to help Schindler. He and his wife, Mila, were at the airport the day Schindler came to Los Angeles in 1965.

It was serendipitous when writer Thomas Keneally walked into the luggage store that the Pages owned in Beverly Hills and became fascinated by the story Mr. Page told him. Page celebrated the publication of Keneally's book *Schindler's Ark* (*Schindler's List* in the United States) in 1982 and contributed valuable insight to the 1993 Steven Spielberg film, *Schindler's List*. Leopold Page died in 2001.

Page's wife, Mila, who was also on the "list,"

is still living and is a dear friend. She is the last surviving founding member of The "1939" Club, an organization of Holocaust survivors, mostly from Poland, and their descendants.

My own life changed with the release of Spielberg's movie *Schindler's List*. Until the film I had remained mostly silent about my past. When there was such enormous interest in the movie, I began rethinking my reluctance to talk about my experiences. Shortly after the movie's release, Dennis McLellan, a reporter for the *Los Angeles Times*, found me through Spielberg's company. He telephoned our house and left a message with his phone number, requesting an interview. I ignored the call for a couple of days until Lis encouraged me to give him the courtesy of a yes or a no. By that time I had made up my mind. I would give him a definite no. I just wasn't ready to do an interview about my Holocaust experiences. Mr. McLellan was a persistent reporter. Too clever and too persistent for me, because by the end of our phone conversation, I had agreed he could come to our house just for a "chat."

One evening he came over after work. As we talked, I quickly was charmed by his sincere interest and concern. When he politely asked if he could use his tape recorder, I saw no reason to object. By then he had my complete confidence. After we talked for several hours, he asked if he could take my picture. I agreed, expecting him to pull out a camera. Instead, he opened our front door and called out, "Okay, you can come in." A photographer, who had arrived with Mr. McLellan hours earlier, stepped inside and snapped several photos of me. The following Sunday, January 23, 1994, my story and my photo ran on the front page of the Orange County edition of the *Los Angeles Times*.

After the article appeared, my students and fellow teachers mobbed me at school. One young man who had not done particularly well in my class came running up to me on campus. He grabbed my hand, shook it, and said, "Mr. Leyson, I'm so glad you made it." I've never forgotten the total genuineness of his response. Friends, students, and teachers asked me why I had never told them about what I had experienced during the war. I didn't have a good answer. Maybe I hadn't really been ready to speak about my experiences until so many years later, or maybe people hadn't really been ready to listen, or maybe both. The outpouring of interest from the community touched me deeply. I began to accept invitations to share my story at churches, synagogues, schools, and political, military, civic, and philanthropic organizations, locally and across the United States and Canada.

In 1995, I met Dr. Marilyn Harran, a professor and the founding director of the Rodgers Center for Holocaust Education at Chapman University in Orange, California. With her encouragement, I began to speak at Chapman and other venues. Chapman has become a second home to me. I will always cherish the memory of the graduation ceremony in 2011, when the university presented me with an honorary doctorate of humane letters. With my wife, my children, my grand-children, and many friends there, it was one of the proudest days of my life. A little boy who had been told he wasn't good enough to go to school was now "Dr. Leyson." I could only imagine the pride my parents would have felt.

They never would have believed that a wonderful television newsman in Los Angeles named Fritz Coleman, who interviewed me at a Hanukkah candle-lighting ceremony, would decide to talk with me some more, and then create a half-hour news special. My story, *A Child on Schindler's List*, was broadcast on KNBC in December 2008. I was thrilled when Fritz and his colleague, Kimber Liponi, won a local Emmy for their work.

I speak often now. My talks are unrehearsed. I never use notes, so each talk is different. I say what I am moved to say. When I speak, I follow the same story you've been reading. It's never easy to recount what I lived through, no matter how many years or how much distance I put between myself and the boy I once was. Each time I speak, I feel again the pain of watching my parents suffer, the cold and hunger of all those nights in Płaszów, and the loss of my two brothers. That moment when Tsalig was torn away from us haunts me every day.

As I've grown older and become a parent myself, my admiration for my own parents and all they did to attempt to protect us has grown even greater as has my admiration for Oskar Schindler. Over the years, from books and documentaries, and especially from my fellow Schindler's "list" survivors, I have learned much more about what Schindler did and how much he hazarded to protect our lives. His accountant, Itzhak Stern, thought that Schindler committed to saving Jews after he witnessed the mass killings during the liquidation of the Kraków ghetto. He was already sympathetic to the plight of his Jewish workers; but from that time on, he increased his efforts to save as many Jews as he could. With money from black market dealings, he bought a piece of land adjacent to his Emalia factory, built the barracks, and persuaded Commandant Goeth with smooth talk and substantial amounts of money that having his workers nearby would increase productivity. His real goal was to rescue his workers from Płaszów and the sadistic Goeth.

Schindler courageously took risks despite the possible dire consequences. He constantly attracted suspicion for his corruption and for his unorthodox treatment of Jews. During the years of unprecedented inhumanity, Schindler saw value in the very people the Nazis labeled as less than human and sought to eradicate. For the most part, he wooed those in authority and those who were surely his enemies by showering them with generous bribes and gifts that were simply too tempting for most high-ranking Nazis, camp commandants, SS officers, and local police to refuse. And he certainly knew how to throw a party.

In 1943, Oskar Schindler was arrested and

briefly jailed for his black market activities. That same year the Nazis threatened to close his factory if he didn't switch from producing enamelware to making armaments. Schindler was forced to agree, but ironically, that change was what saved our lives near the end of the war when Schindler argued that his "expert" workers had to be moved to Brünnlitz. An argument that he had "essential" enamelware workers wouldn't have meant anything to the decision makers, but the argument that we were essential to Germany's munitions production did.

When other German factory owners took their profits and fled Kraków, intent on saving their lives and fortunes, Schindler increased his efforts to save his Jews. Had he not done so, most of us would have died in Auschwitz or other camps. Even though we were close to starving at the end of the time in Brünnlitz, we managed to survive because Schindler chose to spend his fortune on buying us food.

He did everything in his power to protect us.

Thanks to him, it turns out that I didn't die from the last bullet of the war after all.

As a Jewish kid during those times, I fought to live every day. I didn't have a choice. As an influential Nazi, Schindler did have a choice. Countless times he could have abandoned us, taken his fortune, and fled. He could have decided that his life depended on working us to death, but he didn't. Instead, he put his own life in danger every time he protected us for no other reason than it was the right thing to do. I am not a philosopher, but I believe that Oskar Schindler defines heroism. He proves that one person can stand up to evil and make a difference.

I am living proof of that.

I recall a television interview I once saw with scholar and writer Joseph Campbell. I've never forgotten his definition of a hero. Campbell said that a hero is an ordinary human being who does "the best of things in the worst of times." Oskar Schindler personifies that definition.

For years after the war I searched for my brother Tsalig in crowds. I would see a young man who resembled him, and for a split second I would feel a surge of hope. *He has come back,* I thought. *He escaped.* If anyone could do it, my superhero brother could. Each time hope turned into bitter disappointment. Tsalig had not escaped. He did not magically reappear, not in the ghetto, not anywhere. Years later I learned that no one had survived from the transport that took Tsalig and Miriam to Belżec.

My wife, Lis, and I still live in Fullerton, California, where we settled on our sixth anniversary in 1971. Our daughter, Constance (Stacy) Miriam, and her husband, David, live in Virginia and have three sons, Nicholas, Tyler, and Brian. Tyler has the middle name Jacob to honor the memory of my grandfathers. Our son, Daniel, and his wife, Camille, live in Los Angeles and have one daughter, Mia, and twin sons, Benjamin and Silas. Daniel has the middle name Tsalig. So does his son Benjamin.

Both Tsalig's name and something of his spirit live on in them. I am certain of it.

Leon Leyson
September 15, 2012

	H.Art H.Nat.	H.Nr.	N a m e und Vorname	Geburts- datum	Beruf
	Ju.Po.	69077	Allerhand Salo	15. 6.28	Tischlergeh.
	"	8	Becksmann Samuel	12. 7.21	Kutscher
	"	69080	Hilfstein Edward	17. 9.24	Wasserinst.Ge..
	"	1	Altmann Dawid	9. 5.17	Wasserinst.Ge..
	"	2	Dantiger Eduard	16. 2.09	Konstruktions..
	"	3	Beer Alter	11.11.11	ang.Metallver..
	"	4	Bau Josef	18. 6.20	Zeichner/Grap..
	"	5	Bottner Bojzesz	2. 5.18	Tischlermeiste..
	"	6	Preisann Leib	1. 7.05	Schneiderges.
	"	7	Glücksmann Siegfried	30.12.06	Maschinenbaute..
	"	9	Halann Salonon	4. 4.03	Maurer
	"	69090	Binder Alter	21. 3.06	Lackiervermis..
	"	1	Dann Julius	17.10.07	Malerges.
	"	2	Hrathiowics Naten	8. 7.11	Schuhmacherma..
	"	3	Anstübel Dawid	31. 3.09	Stanzer
	Ju.Dt.	4	Beck Friedrich	25. 6.86	Zahnarzt
	Ju.Po.	5	Bachsbaum Jakob	3. 4.21	ang.Metallver..
	"	6	Beder Fischel	15. 6.14	Tischlergeh.
	"	7	Brauner Jersy	23. 7.26	ang.Metallver..
	"	8	Gruber Chaim	4. 5.97	Klempnerges.
	"	9	Blechsisen Mendel	1. 6.06	ang.Metallver..
2	"	69100	Berger Chaim	1. 3.10	Schmiedeges.
	"	1	Dreiblatt Majer	21. 5.09	Maschinentisc..
	"	2	Abeng Emanuel	10. 6.04	Schreibkraft
	"	3	Braun Rafael	9. 6.25	ang.Metallver..
	"	4	Berlinerblau Lewi	25.12.99	Schreibkraft
	"	5	Oestreicher Jakob	7. 5.17	Schlosserges.
	"	6	Bona Naftali	11. 9.13	Tischler
	"	7	Adler Alexander	25. 5.23	ang.Metallver..
	"	8	Bialywlos Alexander	4. 6.23	Glaser
	"	9	Abusch Josef	28.10.12	Maler-Lackiere..
	"	69110	Baldinger Isak	11.11.22	Schlosserges.
	"	1	Herz Dawid	24. 6.25	Wasserinst.Ge..
	"	2	Gurenics Neilech	22. 8.21	ang.Metallver..
	"	3	Blaufeler Jakob	12. 8.09	ang.Metallver..
	"	4	Blatt Henryk	31. 5.20	Kutscher
	"	5	Bringer Dawid	10.10.21	ang.Autoschen..
	"	6	Kornblau Jakob	29. 3.08	ang.Metallver..
	"	7	Goldberg Efroim	3. 4.17	ang.Metallver..
	"	8	Graner Wilhelm	3.12.14	Werkzeugschlos..
	"	9	Groß Oskar	23. 4.14	Maschinenbaui..
	"	69120	Kakuruts Roman	6. 8.17	Schlosserges..
	"	2	Koscher Banja	6. 2.18	Schneiderges.
	"	3	Maber Ignacy	11. 5.15	ang.Metallver..
	"	4	Dortheimer Wigdor	16. 9.18	Maler-Lackiere..
	"	5	Landesdorfer Isak	7. 4.23	ang.Metallver..
	"	6	Friedmann Leon	27. 4.09	Elektrikermei..
	"	7	Lejson Dawid	1. 8.27	Eisendreherge..
	"	8	Lejzon Leib	15. 9.23	Eisendreherge..
	"	9	Lejzon Moses	19.12.98	Eisendreherge..
	"	69130	Glicensstein Abram	16. 4.16	Schlosserges.
	"	1	Hecht Zygmunt	24.10.26	Tischlerges.
	"	2	Linkowski Maurycy	23. 6.05	ang.Metallver..
	"	3	König Jakob	14. 9.16	ang.Metallver..
	"	4	Goldstein Bernard	5. 1.03	ang.Metallver..
	"	5	Geller Motio	18.12.08	Schlosserges.
	"	6	Dresner Jonas	4. 9.23	Autoschlosser..
	"	7	Feigenbaum Ludwig	20.11.24	Autoschlosser..
	"	69140	Malswer Chaim	28.12.05	ang.Metallver..
	"	69141	Dresner Juda	26. 3.93	Stanzer

The Leyson family about 1930 (*from top left, clockwise*): Tsalig, Hershel, Chanah, David, and Pesza.

Previous page: Leon's name (listed as Leib Lejzon) on Schindler's list.

Lwowska 19. The Leyson apartment in the Kraków ghetto was on the second floor.

The shed behind the apartment in the ghetto where Leon hid with his mother and friends.

Leon's 1947 ID for the displaced persons (DP) camp.

From left to right: Leon, Chanah, and Moshe in 1948.

Leon (*second from left*) in the US Army in Georgia in 1951.

Leon at his graduation from California State University Los Angeles in 1958.

Leon (*second from right*) in fedora and Moshe (*third from right*) and unidentified friends in Germany, around 1948.

Lis and Leon's wedding in July 1965.

Oskar Schindler in Israel in the 1960s.

From left to right: Mila Page, Oskar Schindler, Lis, Leon, David, and an unidentified woman at Los Angeles International Airport in the fall of 1965.

Leon, Daniel, and Lis in 1990.

Stacy and Leon in 1985.

Stacy and Leon at Huntington Park
High School's Bring Your Child to
School Day in 1972.

Daniel and Leon in 1987.

Leon at the machine shop at Huntington Park High School in 1963.

From left to right: Lis, Leon, and Pesza in 1985.

Leon holding his DP camp ID in 1995.

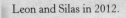
Leon and Silas in 2012.

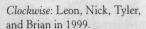
Clockwise: Leon, Nick, Tyler, and Brian in 1999.

Leon and Mia in 2010.

Leon and Ben in 2011.

Leon and Marilyn J. Harran in 2010.

Leon receiving his honorary
doctorate at Chapman
University in 2011.

Leon and David in January 2011
at Gan Shmuel, Israel.

Afterword

Leon Leyson died on January 12, 2013. For more than three years, Leon suffered from T-cell lymphoma. He was stalwart throughout the ordeal. He never lost his kind ways nor his sense of humor. He knew Peter Steinberg had agreed to handle his manuscript, but he did not live to know that Atheneum would publish his book. The driving force that kept Leon telling his story year after year, even though he relived heartbreaking grief each time he spoke, was to honor the memory of his family and of the millions of other victims of the Holocaust. I know he is at peace with the knowledge that in this book, the story of his loved ones, of his hero Oskar Schindler, and of the times of unspeakable evil and stunning courage will live on for generations.

Is seems to me that for those of you who never knew Leon personally, the best way to help you understand the man whose story you just read is to share with you the tributes given by his daughter, Stacy Miriam, and his son, Daniel Tsalig, at the memorial service arranged by Dr. Marilyn Harran at Chapman University on February 17, 2013.

Their words that follow are slightly condensed from the original.

—Elisabeth B. Leyson

From Stacy:

Many people—friends and strangers—have been kind enough to share their wonderful memories of my dad with me—memories of Leon the friend, the uncle, the cousin, the neighbor, the colleague, the teacher. As I heard these and sifted through my own memories, I recognized a common theme, and I realized that if I had to choose one adjective to describe my dad, it would be "generous."

Obviously, he was generous with his story, sharing it with groups around the country. Did he worry how big the group was? No. Did he worry about the group's religious beliefs? No. Did he make any group feel less important to him than another? No. Did he ever ask for or accept money? No!

And he always had time to answer questions and hear comments afterward. He ran over more than once, but few seemed to notice.

He was generous with his birthday. Because of cultural traditions and his rather traumatic childhood, he was not sure of his exact birth date. He had a general idea and chose September 15. The fact that his second grandson was born on that same day in 1994 confirmed to him that he'd picked the right date. My dad always made an effort to be with Tyler Jacob on their shared birthday, often flying across the country.

He was generous with his enthusiasm. He delighted in all the accomplishments of his children, grandchildren, and his children-in-law, no matter how insignificant or ordinary they might have seemed. Whenever we spoke on the phone, one question he never failed to ask was "How is my bagel buddy?" He and his third grandson, Brian, shared a love of bagels.

He loved to hear that a grandchild had learned to sit up or had a new tooth. He loved a musical performance from my sons, even when they were just learning their instruments and, to the rest of us, were not so good. He could make you feel good about something as simple as answering a crossword puzzle clue correctly or teaching your kid to tie his shoe. He was the resident dishwasher at home and also when he came to visit my family. One of my favorite pictures captured him with his hands in a sink full of dishes, smiling like it was the most fun a person could have.

He was generous with his knowledge. He was never too busy to answer a question and explain it until it was understood—even as recently as this past December. My dad had quite a collection of less common measuring devices. My oldest son, Nick, was very curious about a specific one. At this time, my dad was spending most of his time asleep and in his room, trying to find some relief from the almost constant and excruciating pain. Usually, a few times a day, he would feel up to visitors for a short while. One evening, all of us gathered around his bed to take advantage of one of those times, and Nick asked about this mysterious implement. With obvious enjoyment, my dad proceeded to explain the mechanics and uses of the item in a way we could all understand. It seemed to take him away from his reality for a few moments. He told us how to assemble it. He gave examples of how and when to use it. He answered questions. Nick says, "He always had time to answer my questions and seemed to know something about everything." Now, if you ever need to know how to use a dial gauge, you know whom to ask.

My dad was generous with his time. He

taught me to actually tell time and was so proud when once, I asked what time it was and then said, "Never mind, I can look for myself."

Third grade was when we learned multiplication tables. He and I spent a lot of time around the kitchen table together, drilling and drilling. I had some mental block with seven times eight, and we went over it and over it until it finally sunk in. I relived that experience when each of my children learned their tables, and none of us forget the answer is fifty-six.

He also could linger over a hot cup of coffee and made a habit of "taking a little walk" to the nearby Starbucks. My husband shares that borderline unnatural love of Starbucks, and whenever they were in the same town, they would go together, sharing coffee and quality time.

He was especially generous with his laughter. He loved a good joke—and even a bad one. He seemed to have one ready to tell for any occasion. For example, if buttered toast (or something similar) fell with the buttered side down, he loved to say, "I must've buttered the wrong side." He had a beautiful smile, an easy, generous laugh.

He once said, "The truth is, I did not live my life in the shadow of the Holocaust." My dad's experiences during his youth in Europe were extraordinary, but they did not make him the person he was. Not that the experiences didn't have a huge impact; of course they did. But the unenviable events of his young life did not define him: He defined the events. Those childhood experiences only brushed away the youthful luxury of self-centeredness to reveal the character of the man he was always destined to be.

—Stacy Leyson Wilfong

From Daniel:
When my dad died I got very possessive of him. When the rabbis eulogized him at his funeral, I thought, only half jokingly, *Wait a minute—he's mine.* He was more than a witness to Jewish

history. He was my dad. He took me fishing; to Indian Guides; and to soccer, baseball, and basketball practice. He was at all my water polo games. He was a happy guy, and we had a happy life. We laughed a lot.

So here are a few things about him that will help you know my father:

He had a great ear for music and for languages. He learned languages easily and spoke them with a perfect accent, like English (and Yiddish, Polish, Hebrew, German, Russian well enough that some Soviet soldiers during the Soviet occupation of Kraków arrested him as a Russian deserter, Hungarian well enough that Hungarian acquaintances in the DP camp thought he was Hungarian, some Czech, some Japanese, and some Spanish).

He tolerated most of my musical phases. He liked most of the bands I liked, and we would talk about the meaning of song lyrics. We always agreed that we liked songs in minor keys. I think minor keys reminded him of the old country.

He was a black belt in judo, a pretty good tennis player, and an excellent bowler, with a mean left-handed hook.

He told me the first sip of beer was the best. "If they could just bottle the first sip," he said. Later, I thought, *They do bottle the first sip, don't they?*

He told me he didn't know anything until he was fifty. From my perspective, he seemed to know how everything worked and could fix anything. He also had the right advice for every situation. He pretty much taught me everything I know about anything worthwhile, like how to approach seemingly insurmountable tasks. "Just keep your head down and go to work," he told me. Now that he's gone, I wish I had listened more, because he had a lot of knowledge of all kinds, and it came from his unique life experiences.

He liked coffee. Black. A lot.

His favorite piece of advice to me was: "Don't be dumb." Good advice. I did a lot of dumb things growing up. Still do. Case in point:

A few months ago my dad came over when I was working around the house. My daughter's closet door was rubbing on the carpet, so I decided I would trim the bottom of it with an electric saw he had just given me. I was feeling pretty good about myself as I carried the door out to the garage. "Make a notch in it," he told me. *I thought, I know which end of the door is the top; I don't need a notch.* Of course, I cut the wrong end of the door off, so now there is a huge gap at the top of the door. And the cut isn't straight either. He gave me a hard time about that until the end. But his last comment to me about it before he died was, quietly, "It's okay. You know how many times I've done that?"

I suppose it's normal for young adults to want to be different from their parents. There was a time when I was like that. But I am no longer a young adult, and as I watched him in his hospice bed, I just kept thinking to myself, *I want to be as much like him as I possibly can.* He was such a special guy, he can't just disappear. The best I can hope for at this point is to live a life that would make him proud. I'll try to do that.

—Daniel Leyson

Acknowledgments

Not once, not in 1994 when he spoke to an audience for the first time nor in his numerous presentations over the next eighteen years— sometimes averaging one per week—did Leon use notes. He relied on the question sessions following his speeches, the informal conversations with the many who lingered to hug or have their photos taken with him, the videos made at a number of venues, and the hundreds of letters from students to help him revise and clarify the essence of his story. He wanted to make sure the same question wasn't repeated at another event. Over the years, a definite core of content emerged that became the foundation for this book. But there was little on paper.

Leon spoke throughout the United States and Canada. In every instance, there was immense interest in his experiences. We are grateful to each of you who attended his talks. Your sensitivity and kindness gave Leon the courage and stamina to continue telling his story, even as his health was deteriorating.

The Fullerton community where Leon lived for over forty years was especially supportive; your positive response confirmed for him the value of his story. California Assemblymember and former Fullerton mayor Sharon Quirk-Silva recognized Leon for his contributions to the community and local schools and honored his memory at the state assembly's Holocaust Remembrance Day in Sacramento on April 8, 2013.

Leon's many friends helped him immeasurably as he first began to deal with the painful memories of his childhood. Many of you attended numerous presentations and invited him to speak at your community organization or place of worship. Your empathy encouraged Leon to continue, even though each time he told his story, he relived the anguish of those years of peril and grief.

Several educators in southern California invited Leon to speak at their school or university every year for nearly fifteen years. These opportunities played an essential role in the development of this book. Special thanks go to Irene Strauss of Parks Junior High School; Bob Jensen, Doreen Villasenor, and Vince White of Fullerton College; Dr. Sy Scheinberg of California State University of Fullerton; and Dr. James Brown of Chapman University. Your confidence in Leon strengthened his.

After each presentation, the most repeated comment was that Leon should write a book. He replied, "I'm working on it," but there was not much progress until Emily Scott, a Holocaust history minor at Chapman University, interviewed Leon and compiled her notes as her senior project. Emily's commitment and enthusiasm touched Leon deeply.

Following a presentation at the Great Vest Side Club in Chicago, Louis Weber, publisher of *The Holocaust Chronicle* and CEO of Publications

International, urged Leon to write of his experience in the Holocaust. Mr. Weber provided the names and résumés of several professional writers who might help Leon organize the content. Leon hired Sophie Sartain, with whom he worked for over a year. Sophie recorded conversations with Leon and produced an outstanding record of Leon's history. Her skillful questioning enabled Leon to add significant details to the topics he could only touch on in his ninety-minute presentations.

Additional thanks go to the administration of Chapman University, particularly President James L. Doti and Chancellor Daniele Struppa for championing Holocaust education as a vital component of the university's curriculum. Jessica MyLymuk, Ashley Bloomfield, and Joyce Greenspan of the Rodgers Center for Holocaust Education at Chapman University, and research associate Jeff Koerber, gave crucial support to this project. Thanks go to the many Chapman colleagues, friends, and members of the Rodgers Center Board of Visitors for their unfailing encouragement.

ACKNOWLEDGMENTS

Our gratitude goes to David M. Crowe, author of *Oskar Schindler: The Untold Account of His Life, Wartime Activities, and the True Story Behind "The List,"* who generously shared his knowledge with Marilyn. We want to thank Dr. Jan Osborn and Tom Zoellner of the English department at Chapman University. Dr. Osborn provided astute recommendations for an early draft of the manuscript. Tom, an accomplished author, offered expert advice and mentored Marilyn in preparing the formal proposal.

During the period when Leon's health grew more and more fragile, Tom sent the proposal to Peter Steinberg of the Peter Steinberg Agency. Peter immediately recognized the value of the story and contacted Caitlyn Dlouhy, vice president and editorial director at Atheneum Books at Simon & Schuster Publishers, and in Peter's words, "the best editor of young adult books in the country." Thank you, Peter, for your enthusiasm and your expertise.

Within two days of receiving the manuscript,

Atheneum made an offer to publish the book, giving us the priceless opportunity to work with Caitlyn. Peter was right. She *is* the best in the business. Caitlyn's thoroughness, diplomacy, perceptiveness, and patience have guided us through the revision process. No one could ask for a more dedicated guide. Thank you, Caitlyn. Your belief in the value of Leon's story is (almost) as strong as ours.

We also want to thank Dan Potash, who designed the jacket and the layout of the book. The artwork complements the context with just the right combination of reality and suggestion. Thanks also to Jeannie Ng. She excelled as a managing editor, a job that requires intense attention to detail and a gentle handling of the writer.

Leon's extended family in California, Virginia, Oregon, New Mexico, and Israel were valuable resources for information and for accuracy. You reached out to Leon as he struggled with the sadness of his childhood and youth, and did everything possible to make sure Leon's "real" life was brimming with love and happiness. Thank you for showing your affection for Leon in so many ways. Special thanks go to Beaty Kaufman and Anne Ambers, and to Camille Hahn Leyson for her assistance on several drafts.

I [Lis] thank Su Grossman, my sister. Su provided comfort, guidance, enthusiasm, and sustenance to Leon and me during the years Leon and I were working on this book. Her generosity has no limits.

To Stacy and Dan and their spouses, Dave and Camille, and to Nick, Tyler, Brian, Mia, Benjamin, and Silas: Just being you was the most significant, ever present, guiding light for Leon. In each of you, his spirit lives on.

—Marilyn J. Harran
and Elisabeth B. Leyson

Resources

To learn more about the Holocaust, you can visit these sites:

The Rodgers Center for Holocaust Education, Chapman University
chapman.edu/holocausteducation

United States Holocaust Memorial Museum
ushmm.org

USC Shoah Foundation—
The Institute for Visual History and Education
sfi.usc.edu

The "1939" Club
1939club.com

Yad Vashem
yadvashem.org